Frommer's®

W9-BSX-166

Yosemite and Sequoia & King Canyon National Parks

5th Edition

by Eric Peterson

Here's what critics say about Frommer's:

"Amazingly easy to use. Very portable, very complete."

—*Booklist*

"Detailed, accurate, and easy-to-read information for all price ranges."

—*Glamour Magazine*

WILEY

Wiley Publishing, Inc.

Published by:

WILEY PUBLISHING, INC.
111 River St.
Hoboken, NJ 07030-5774

ISBN-13: 978-0-471-76989-7
ISBN-10: 0-471-76989-4

Editor: Elizabeth Heath
Production Editor: Eric T. Schroeder
Photo Editor: Richard Fox
Cartographer: Anton Crane
Production by Wiley Indianapolis Composition Services

For information on our other products and services or to obtain technical
support, please contact our Customer Care Department within the U.S. at
800/762-2974, outside the U.S. at 317/572-3993 or fax 317/572-4002.

Wiley also publishes its books in a variety of electronic formats. Some con-
tent that appears in print may not be available in electronic formats.

Manufactured in the United States of America

5   4   3   2   1

Contents

List of Maps

ABOUT THE AUTHOR

A Denver-based freelance writer, **Eric Peterson** has written and contributed to numerous Frommer's guides covering the American West, from Montana to Texas. He has also recently written several coffee-table books and *Ramble: A Field Guide to the USA* (www.speckpress.com). He likes to hike in the Rockies, ride his cruiser around Denver, and walk his faithful mutt, Giblet.

AN INVITATION TO THE READER

In researching this book, we discovered many wonderful places—hotels, restaurants, shops, and more. We're sure you'll find others. Please tell us about them, so we can share the information with your fellow travelers in upcoming editions. If you were disappointed with a recommendation, we'd love to know that, too. Please write to:

Frommer's Yosemite and Sequoia & Kings Canyon National Parks,
5th Edition
Wiley Publishing, Inc. • 111 River St. • Hoboken, NJ 07030-5774

AN ADDITIONAL NOTE

Please be advised that travel information is subject to change at any time—and this is especially true of prices. We therefore suggest that you write or call ahead for confirmation when making your travel plans. The authors, editors, and publisher cannot be held responsible for the experiences of readers while traveling. Your safety is important to us, however, so we encourage you to stay alert and be aware of your surroundings. Keep a close eye on cameras, purses, and wallets, all favorite targets of thieves and pickpockets.

FROMMER'S STAR RATINGS, ICONS & ABBREVIATIONS

Every hotel, restaurant, and attraction listing in this guide has been ranked for quality, value, service, amenities, and special features using a **star-rating system.** In country, state, and regional guides, we also rate towns and regions to help you narrow down your choices and budget your time accordingly. Hotels and restaurants are rated on a scale of zero (recommended) to three stars (exceptional). Attractions, shopping, nightlife, towns, and regions are rated according to the following scale: zero stars (recommended), one star (highly recommended), two stars (very highly recommended), and three stars (must-see).

In addition to the star-rating system, we also use **seven feature icons** that point you to the great deals, in-the-know advice, and unique experiences that separate travelers from tourists. Throughout the book, look for:

Finds	Special finds—those places only insiders know about
Fun Fact	Fun facts—details that make travelers more informed and their trips more fun
Kids	Best bets for kids—advice for the whole family
Moments	Special moments—those experiences that memories are made of
Overrated	Places or experiences not worth your time or money
Tips	Insider tips—some great ways to save time and money
Value	Great values—where to get the best deals

The following abbreviations are used for credit cards:

AE	American Express	DISC	Discover	V	Visa
DC	Diners Club	MC	MasterCard		

FROMMERS.COM

Now that you have the guidebook to a great trip, visit our website at www.frommers.com for travel information on more than 3,000 destinations. With features updated regularly, we give you instant access to the most current trip-planning information available. At Frommers.com, you'll also find the best prices on airfares, accommodations, and car rentals—and you can even book travel online through our travel booking partners. At Frommers.com, you'll also find the following:

- Online updates to our most popular guidebooks
- Vacation sweepstakes and contest giveaways
- Newsletter highlighting the hottest travel trends
- Online travel message boards with featured travel discussions

Introduction to Yosemite and Sequoia & Kings Canyon National Parks

California's Sierra Nevada imposes rugged features on a state that many associate with sandy beaches and palm trees. It's a mountain range of great beauty, hidden amid harsh wilderness, and nowhere is the terrain more dramatic than in Yosemite and Sequoia & Kings Canyon National Parks. Both combine mountains with meadows, waterfalls with wildflowers, and spectacular geology with awe-inspiring vistas that span, in some cases, nearly the breadth of the state. Together, these parks cover 1.6 million acres (roughly 2,520 sq. miles). They host approximately 6 million visitors a year and are home to thousands of species of plants and animals.

Yosemite attracts more tourists than Sequoia & Kings Canyon, although all three are absolutely delightful parks. Yosemite covers 1,169 square miles—roughly the size of Rhode Island—and 94% is designated wilderness. Here you can enjoy the quiet beauty of a forest or a pristine meadow, observe a sunset from a towering granite cliff, hike a half-mile-high waterfall, enjoy a moonlit night that's as bright as day, climb a world-famous rock, and eat a gourmet meal before falling asleep—be it under the stars or in the luxurious bed of a top-rated hotel.

Yosemite Valley, which attracts 95% of all Yosemite tourists, is just a sliver of the park, but it holds a number of the region's jaw-dropping features. An average of 4.1 million people visit here each year. It is a place of record-setting statistics: the highest waterfall in North America and three of the tallest in the world (Upper Yosemite, Sentinel, and Ribbon falls); and the biggest and tallest piece of exposed granite (El Capitan).

Wawona, a small community annexed to the park in 1932, is a 45-minute drive south of Yosemite Valley. Mostly a hodgepodge of resort cabins and private homes, Wawona is also home to the stately

Yosemite National Park

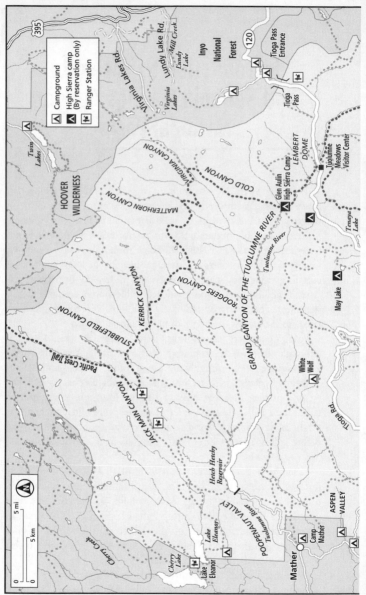

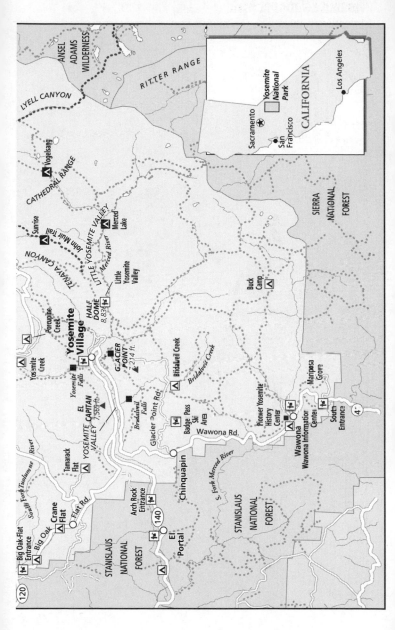

Sequoia & Kings Canyon National Parks

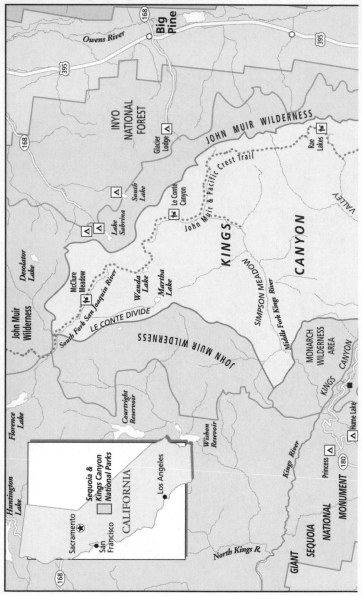

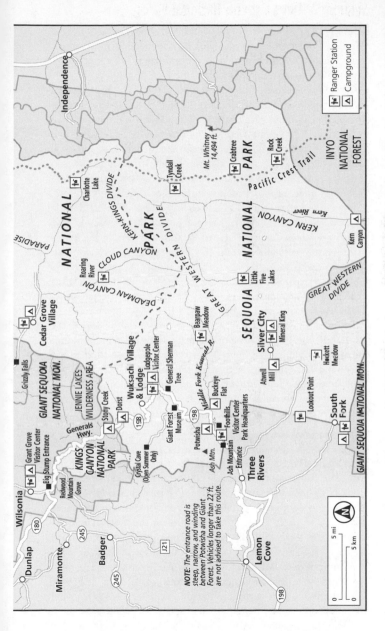

NOTE: The entrance road is steep, narrow, and winding between Potwisha and Giant Forest. Vehicles longer than 22 ft. are not advised to take this route.

Ranger Station

Campground

5

Wawona Hotel, a nine-hole golf course, and a main attraction—the Mariposa Grove, the largest grove of giant sequoias in Yosemite. There are two smaller groves located near Crane Flat, about a half-hour drive west of Yosemite Valley.

Yosemite National Park's Tuolumne Meadows, an immense plateau peppered with wildflowers during the summer, and the glimmering Tuolumne River are an hour-and-a-half drive northeast of the valley. Tuolumne Meadows is surrounded by a half dozen domes and peaks. The high country also includes White Wolf Lodge, Tenaya Lake, and Tuolumne Meadows Lodge. The two lodges are little more than restaurants with a collection of tent-cabins. All of these, plus backcountry outposts accessible only on foot, are described in chapter 5, "Where to Stay & Eat in Yosemite."

In the heart of the Sierra Nevada, just south of Yosemite, are Sequoia & Kings Canyon National Parks, home to both the largest giant sequoia trees in the world and a deep gorge of a canyon that rivals Yosemite Valley for awe-inspiring beauty. Sequoia & Kings Canyon are separate parks snuggled next to one another and managed jointly. Combined, they outsize Yosemite. Peaks stretch across 1,350 square miles and include 14,494-foot Mount Whitney, the tallest point in the lower 48 states. These parks are also home to the Kaweah Range, a string of stark and magnificently beautiful mountains nestled among the Sierras. Three powerful rivers, the Kings, Kern, and Kaweah, tumble through the parks. Despite their large size, Sequoia & Kings Canyon National Parks attract less than half the number of Yosemite's annual visitors, making them an appreciated alternative for those looking to avoid huge crowds.

1 History of the Region

This region of the Sierra Nevada has a rich natural and cultural history. The landscape can change completely from one mile to the next. High mountain meadows give way to turbulent rivers that thunder down deep gorges, tumble over vast waterfalls, and turn into wide, shallow rivers as they meander through the next valley. Such diversity can be attributed to the region's geologic roots, which stretch back 10 to 80 million years when a head-on collision between two immense plates of rock formed this mountain range. The rock, weakened by extreme temperature variations, was later carved by erosion into deep valleys, including Yosemite Valley and Kings Canyon. In a process described more fully in chapter 9, "A Nature Guide to Yosemite and Sequoia & Kings Canyon National Parks," the Ice Age brought glaciers that smoothed the faces of rocks such as Yosemite's El Capitan and Half Dome, some of the towering peaks of Yosemite's Tuolumne Meadows, and Kings Canyon itself.

American Indians were aware of Yosemite at least 5,000 years ago. While Egyptian scholars were making their first use of numbers, American Indians in California were living as their forebears had for thousands of years. By 1000 B.C., there were tribes—including the Ahwahneeches (Ah-*wah*-nee-ches), a sub-tribe of the Miwok—living in Yosemite Valley. Archaeologists have since documented 36 living sites on the valley floor that supported a vast number of inhabitants with lush vegetation and numerous animals. The largest village lay just below Yosemite Falls.

Despite the fact that the early inhabitants were called Ahwahneeches, the valley was named Yosemite by soldiers sent to oust American Indians who refused to relocate to the plains. While seated around a campfire, a doctor among the group suggested the soldiers settle on a name for the valley. Among the suggestions were Paradise Valley and Yosemite, the name by which the Indian tribes in the region were known. Some were offended by the suggestion of honoring American Indians in the valley, but in the end, the name Yosemite won. Ironically, however, Yosemite was the soldiers' mispronunciation of the word Oo-*hoo*-ma-te, the name of just one settlement of Ahwahneeches, whom soldiers drove from Yosemite Valley in 1851.

The Ahwahneeches' neighbors, the Monaches (also known as the Western Monos), lived in Kings Canyon and met their end during a smallpox outbreak in 1862. The Monaches kept villages in the foothills all year long, although they sometimes moved to the forest in the summer. The Potwishas and Wuksachis were sub-tribes of the Monaches who also lived in the foothills, around Sequoia's Ash Mountain. In today's park, there's a campground called Potwisha and a motel named Wuksachi. Kings Canyon was named in 1806 by the Spaniard Gabriel Moraga—the first European to lead an expedition in these parts. Moraga's party discovered a major river on January 6, the Roman Catholic day of the Epiphany. Being a good Catholic, Moraga christened the river El Río de los Santos Reyes, or "the river of the holy kings," in honor of the three wise men who visited the infant Jesus on the same date, albeit many years earlier. The name was later shortened to Kings River.

The land of Kings Canyon and Sequoia remained untouched until 1827, when trappers arrived. The California gold rush drew

Impressions

The clearest way into the universe is through a forest wilderness.

—Author and naturalist John Muir, 1938

hordes more in 1849, and abandoned mines dot Sequoia & Kings Canyon National Parks, especially in Mineral King, a region unsuccessfully mined for silver in the 1800s.

Despite being plagued by natural upheavals such as prehistoric earthquakes and glaciers, Yosemite, Sequoia, and Kings Canyon survived. Then the parks faced another challenge—each was destined for destruction by dams, logging, and consequent flooding. Large stands of giant sequoia were obliterated in the late 1800s. Ranchers allowed their sheep to graze beneath the big trees. Sawmills were built, and zip-zip—down came entire forests. Adding insult to injury is the fact that the wood of the largest giant sequoias is brittle and generally pretty useless. Nevertheless, early loggers chopped down a third of the ancient trees in the region. This travesty would likely have continued if not for a few mid-19th-century conservationists, who pushed the government to turn the areas into parks. In 1890, Sequoia National Park was created, along with the tiny General Grant National Park, established to protect Grant Grove. Unfortunately, the move was too late to spare Converse Basin. Once the largest stand of giant sequoias in the world, today it's a cemetery of tree stumps, the grave markers of fallen giants.

In 1926, the park was expanded eastward to include the small Kern Canyon and Mount Whitney, but rumblings continued over the fate of Kings Canyon itself. For a while, its future lay as a reservoir. It wasn't until the 1960s that Kings Canyon was finally protected for good. In 1978, Mineral King was added to Sequoia's half of the park. The parks have been managed jointly since World War II.

While the fight to save the giant sequoias raged, a similar battle was taking place over Yosemite. Here the threat came from opportunists hoping to cash in on Yosemite Valley's beauty. Soon after the Ahwahneeches were driven out, homesteaders came in. They built hotels and crude homes and planted row crops and orchards. Somehow, during the Civil War, Congress convinced President Abraham Lincoln to sign legislation protecting the valley and the nearby Mariposa Grove of giant sequoias. Yosemite Valley was, in effect, the first state and national park in America. But the thousands of acres surrounding these relatively small federal holdings were still subject to exploitation in the form of mining, logging, and grazing. Happily, on October 1, 1890, a week after approving Sequoia National Park, Congress established Yosemite National Park. The new park did not include the valley or Mariposa Grove, which were still part of the older Yosemite Valley Park, but it encompassed enormous tracts of surrounding wilderness. With two administrations—one overseeing the valley and big trees, and one overseeing the new park—the expected overlap occurred and frustration mounted. In 1906, legislators decided to add the valley and big trees to the new park and to reduce the park's size to follow the natural contours of the land, while excluding private mining and logging operations. Everyone was set to live happily ever after. No one would have predicted that Yosemite would become one of the most popular places on the planet. (Some argue that tourism has accomplished the destruction that logging couldn't.)

Recent years have brought a sense of foreboding to this wilderness haven. Take one trip during peak season and you'll understand why. Traffic backs up for miles; trees and branches along the Merced River become clotheslines; and candy wrappers, cigarette butts, and other paper products litter the valley. The songbirds can barely be heard over the din of voices yelling and hooting. This is the biggest challenge facing Yosemite, and to a far lesser extent Sequoia & Kings Canyon, today. Big changes are expected as the National Park Service grapples with the best way to permit access without causing more irreparable damage to this natural wonderland.

Who would have thought that preservation would wreak its own brand of havoc here? But we can only imagine how this beautiful place would look today had it been left in the hands of profiteers.

2 The Parks Today

In Yosemite, rock slides and torrential flooding in the mid-1990s forever changed the park's appearance; but to be fair, we have to admit that human influence has had an even greater impact. Attendance has doubled in the past 20 years, and now more than 4 million people visit Yosemite annually; in the summer, the average daily census hits 20,000! The major difficulty facing park officials today, due to the park's increasing popularity, is balancing humanity's access to Yosemite's wonders with the need to maintain and improve the park's health. The National Park Service issued a master plan in 2000, aimed at reducing vehicle traffic in Yosemite Valley. Parts of this plan have already been put into effect, and additional changes are planned that will somewhat limit access, especially personal vehicle access, to the park. Many who love Yosemite say this is a small price to pay to protect a treasure.

It's a far different scenario at Sequoia & Kings Canyon National Parks. They get crowded in summer, too, when RVs and slow drivers can turn into a convoy dozens of cars long—but it's nothing like Yosemite. Sequoia & Kings Canyon are much less developed, and the spots that are developed are much more spread out. Frankly, officials here have learned a lesson from Yosemite and work hard not to make the same mistakes. The park is awe-inspiring, with voluptuous canyons and some of the most spectacular trees and vistas in the Sierra, but they are not all crammed into a 7-mile valley, and you won't find a crowd three deep jostling for a view, as in Yosemite.

Crowds aside, there's a movement at both Yosemite and Sequoia & Kings Canyon to return the parks to a more natural state. Nowhere is this more evident than in Yosemite Valley, where nature is forcing officials to make changes long planned but never implemented. For the past 20 years, Yosemite National Park had been governed in part by a general plan that called for restoring meadows, phasing out some campgrounds, and moving others away from waterways to reduce the human impact on rivers, streams, and wildlife. However, little progress had been made. Then in January 1997, during one of the valley's swanky annual winter events, nature took charge.

What began as a torrential downpour turned into one of the most destructive winter storms on record, and when the rain stopped several days later, Yosemite Valley was Yosemite Lake. Swollen streams and creeks swept tons of debris—trees, rocks, brush—into the valley, clogging the Merced River. Campgrounds were submerged, employees' quarters were flooded, and much of Yosemite Lodge was under 2 feet of water. Despite frantic attempts at sandbagging, hundreds of people were forced onto higher ground—the top floors of buildings—and everyone was stuck. The water was so high and so ferocious that it washed out the roads and stranded about 2,000 people in the valley, including the several hundred on hand to celebrate New Year's Eve. So much was damaged that the valley closed for almost 3 months, and, even after it was reopened, travel was restricted for several months to the park's all-weather highway alone. Although park workers managed to clean most of the fallen trees, boulders, and rocks out of the heavily populated areas in the valley by mid-1997, some backcountry trail bridges were never repaired, and a decision was made to reconsider rebuilding the hundreds of lost campsites.

The storms remind us of the history behind these parks. Millions of years of water, snow, and glaciers have carved the unique canyons of Yosemite Valley and Kings Canyon. So the folks who live here do so with a measure of understanding: They're living at the mercy of nature.

Before this event, officials at both Yosemite and Sequoia & Kings Canyon were already on their way to making some other notable changes. Both parks are renovating and reconstructing. Some meadows are off-limits to foot traffic so that grass and wildflowers can return. When new buildings are constructed, their architecture is designed to reflect or work with the natural surroundings: A restaurant in Yosemite has a wall of glass windows that looks out at Yosemite Falls; a new gift store doubles during the winter as a cross-country ski lodge. In both cases, new structures replaced existing ones, so the impact on pristine wilderness was minimal.

In Sequoia & Kings Canyon, park officials are now putting the finishing touches on a sequoia forest restoration project that they have been working on for the past 16 years. Most of the project's aims affect Giant Forest, one of the most notable stands of trees in Sequoia National Park. Old buildings have been torn down, and roads and parking lots have been moved in an effort to return this area of the park to a more natural state. The goal is ecological restoration—to cease damaging the sequoias' root systems, repair the topsoil, plant sequoia seedlings, and get out of the way while Mother Nature does her thing. An added benefit is that without the buildings this area is more attractive.

Interestingly, park officials also hope that natural fires will return to the area once the heavy human impact is reduced. Fires are an important part of the sequoia's life. The bark of the giant trees is fire resistant, but a blaze will dry out the sequoia's cones, which then open, dropping seeds onto the fire-cleared ground, which is, conveniently, the preferred growth medium for seedlings.

3 The Best of Yosemite and Sequoia & Kings Canyon

It's hard to pick the best of anything, and it's especially difficult to declare something "best" when nature is involved. There are so many heart-thumping hikes, roaring waterfalls, and mind-blowing vistas to explore in these parks that it's almost impossible to pick our favorites. That being said, we're ready with a few suggestions.

THE BEST VIEWS

- **The Panorama from Tunnel View Outside Yosemite Valley:** If you're approaching the park on CA 41 from Wawona, this amazing panorama will sneak up on you, offering a breathtaking surprise. There's plenty of space in the two parking lots to pull over and look. See "Orientation" in chapter 3.

- **Yosemite Valley from Glacier Point:** The easy drive to the top of Glacier Point (open summer only) will leave you speechless. From here, you'll get an eye-level view of the great rocks, such as Half Dome, North Dome, and Cloud's Rest. The stunning valley and waterfalls are spread far below. See chapter 3.

- **Mist Falls from the Bottom in Kings Canyon:** Standing at the base of this waterfall, you'll really appreciate its force, especially during spring and early summer when it's fed by the snowmelt. The crashing of water onto the rocks below drowns out all other noise, and there are rainbows galore. Keep back from the slippery rocks at its edge! See chapters 6 and 7.

THE BEST CAR CAMPGROUNDS

- **North Pines Campground in Yosemite Valley:** Smaller and slightly more isolated than neighboring campgrounds, North Pines offers a true forest camping experience that makes it the most enjoyable of Yosemite Valley's car campgrounds. See p. 77.

- **Buckeye Flat Campground in Sequoia:** This is a small, especially pretty, and secluded campground in the foothills, with a prime location amid a grove of oaks. The only downfall is that it can get very hot in the summer. See p. 133.

- **Sunset Campground in Kings Canyon:** Spread over a rolling hilltop beneath tall trees, this is a peaceful place that glows late into the evening as the sun goes down. It offers some nicely secluded sites, and it's in a good location to hike to some of the park's most impressive big trees. See p. 133.

THE BEST PRIMITIVE CAMPGROUNDS

- **Yosemite Creek:** Just outside Yosemite Valley on CA 120, you'll find this great out-of-the-way campground. It lacks amenities but is far enough off the beaten path to offer solitude. Few venture down the 5-mile dirt road to this campground, but those who do tend to prefer roughing it. See p. 78.

- **South Fork Campground in Sequoia:** This is the smallest developed campsite in the park. It's just inside the park's boundary, set at 3,650 feet along the south fork of the beautiful Kaweah River. See p. 133.
- **Atwell Mill Campground in Sequoia:** The site is situated along Atwell Creek near the east fork of the Kaweah River in the Mineral King region of the park. You'll need time and patience to reach it—allow at least an hour for the 20-mile drive—but it's well worth it. See p. 133.

THE BEST DAY HIKES

- **Vernal Fall in Yosemite:** A must-see for anyone with the stamina. It's just 3 miles round-trip if you follow the Mist Trail, but it requires a strong heart and enough gumption to make the last quarter-mile, ascending 500 stairs. Once at the top, hikers are rewarded with fabulous views and enough space to lounge around like marmots in the sun before the hike back down. See p. 45.
- **Moro Rock in Sequoia:** A short but steep climb up a historic staircase that snakes through rock crevices to the top of Moro Rock. Rewards include one of the most awe-inspiring views in the Sierra Nevada. The walk offers plenty of places to rest on the way up. See p. 111.
- **Mist Falls in Kings Canyon:** This 8-mile round-trip hike climbs 1,500 feet to the spectacular Mist Falls. Along the way, the hiking ranges from moderately strenuous to easy strolling through woodland areas that have lots of places where you can catch your breath. See p. 115.

THE BEST HIGH-COUNTRY HIKES

- **May Lake in Yosemite:** This is an easy 2.5-mile hike that begins near Tioga Road, east of White Wolf (accessible by motor vehicle in summer only). This picturesque walk offers fishing but no swimming. May Lake is dead center in Yosemite National Park. It's a good place to survey surrounding peaks, including the 10,855-foot-high Mount Hoffman rising behind the lake. See p. 52.
- **The High Sierra Trail in Sequoia:** This popular backpacking trail offers day hikers a glimpse of what's out there. It's a moderate, 10-mile hike with pretty views of the middle fork of the Kaweah River and the Kaweah Range. See p. 123.

- **Paradise Valley in Kings Canyon:** This hike extends beyond Mist Falls to a broad valley bisected by a welcoming river. The long 14-mile round-trip hike is a bit much to do in 1 day, but it is possible with some planning and an early start. See p. 116.

THE BEST MEALS

- **Ahwahnee Dining Room in Yosemite Valley:** No surprise here—it's a knockout feast. Every course is almost worth its weight in gold, which is about what it'll cost you, too. See p. 83.
- **Mountain Room Restaurant in Yosemite Valley:** Some people like the Mountain Room even better than the top-rated Ahwahnee. Not only is the food here top-notch, but you also can't beat the views of Yosemite Falls. See p. 85.
- **Wawona Hotel Dining Room in Yosemite:** Located outside the valley, this spacious restaurant is a favorite of locals for miles around. The excellent chef concocts delectable meals, and the views through the expanse of windows provide food for the soul. See p. 86.

THE BEST PLACES FOR REFLECTION

- **Yosemite's Glacier Point at Night:** You're sure to be quietly overwhelmed, either by the number of stars or the way the moonlight reflects off the granite domes surrounding the valley. See chapters 3 and 4.
- **Tenaya Lake in Yosemite:** The solitude and beauty of this high-altitude, crystal-clear lake (accessible by road in summer only) outshines others in the park. Tenaya Lake is larger and more dramatic, edging up against an iridescent granite landscape. See chapters 3 and 4.

2

Planning Your Trip to Yosemite and Sequoia & Kings Canyon National Parks

In the pages that follow, you'll find all the information you need before setting off on your adventure to one of these spectacular National Parks.

1 Getting Started: Information & Reservations

There are reams of visitor information available by phone, in bookstores, and on the Internet for these parks, but the National Park Service is the best place to start.

FOR YOSEMITE

If you're planning a visit to Yosemite National Park, you can get general information on accommodations, weather, and permits from their touch-tone phone menu at © **209/372-0200** or online at **www.nps.gov/yose**. The hearing-impaired can get information by calling © **209/372-4726**. For camping reservations, call © **800/ 436-7275.**

You can buy books and maps from the nonprofit **Yosemite Association,** P.O. Box 230, El Portal, CA 95318 (© **209/379-2646;** www.yosemite.org). For information on much of the lodging within Yosemite National Park, contact **DNC Parks & Resorts at Yosemite,** 5410 E. Home Ave., Fresno, CA 93727 (© **559/252-4848;** www.yosemitepark.com).

Information on lodging and activities outside the park is available from the visitor centers and chambers of commerce in the park's surrounding cities. If you're coming from the west on CA 120, contact the **Tuolumne County Visitor Center** in Sonora (© **800/446-1333** or 209/533-4420; www.thegreatunfenced.com) or the **Highway 120 (CA 120) Chamber of Commerce** in Groveland (© **800/ 449-9120** or 209/962-0429; www.groveland.org). On CA 140, contact the **Mariposa County Visitors Bureau** (© 866/425-3366 or 209/966-3685; www.homeofyosemite.com). On CA 41 south of the park, call the **Yosemite Sierra Visitors Bureau** in Oakhurst (© **559/683-4636;** http://www.yosemitethisyear.com). From Lee Vining on the park's eastern boundary, contact the **Lee Vining Chamber of Commerce** (© 760/647-6629; www.leevining.com). There's a **California Welcome Center** at 710 W. 16th St., Merced (© **800/446-5353** or 209/384-7092; www.yosemite-gateway.org).

FOR SEQUOIA & KINGS CANYON

Start your search at the National Park Service website at **www. nps.gov/seki** for the most up-to-date information on the park, lodging, hikes, regulations, and the best times to visit. Much of the same information, plus road conditions, is available by phone (© 559/565-3341). You can also get a variety of books and maps from the **Sequoia Natural History Association,** 47050 Generals Hwy. #10, Three Rivers, CA 93271 (© **559/565-3759;** www. sequoiahistory.org).

For lodging information and reservations at Wuksachi Lodge in the Giant Forest area of Sequoia National Park, call © **888/252-5757** or 559/565-4070, or surf **www.visitsequoia.com.** In Kings Canyon National Park, call © **559/335-5500** or visit **www. sequoia-kingscanyon.com** for lodging information at Grant Grove, John Muir, or Cedar Grove lodges.

Camping in Sequoia & Kings Canyon is often much easier than in Yosemite, as most of the 14 campgrounds operate on a first-come, first-served basis. To get up-to-date information, call the general Sequoia & Kings Canyon information line at © **559/565-3341.**

2 When to Go

Both Yosemite and Sequoia & Kings Canyon are open year-round.

YOSEMITE   Avoid holiday weekends in spring and summer if possible—park campgrounds are usually full June through August—and expect some crowds in late spring and early fall as well. Winter is a great time to visit Yosemite—not only is the park virtually empty, but there are a number of activities, from downhill skiing and sledding at Badger Pass, to cross-country skiing, snow-shoeing, and even ice skating. Keep in mind that the high country along Tioga and Glacier Point roads is inaccessible to motor vehicles from mid-fall to early June, when weather closes the roads.

SEQUOIA & KINGS CANYON   Like Yosemite, a variety of attractions stay open at these parks all year, but Cedar Grove is closed from mid-November to mid-April and Mineral King is closed from November 1 until Memorial Day weekend. Summertime sees a lively population of adventure seekers (see chapter 7, "Hikes & Other Outdoor Pursuits in Sequoia & Kings Canyon"). The hiking trail passes in the high country may be snowbound until July.

CLIMATE

The climate at both Yosemite and Sequoia & Kings Canyon varies considerably, depending on the region of the park. A good rule of thumb is to remember that the higher you go, the cooler it gets. So pack a parka on any trip that climbs above the valley floor or ventures into the backcountry.

In summer, temperatures at lower elevations (such as Yosemite Valley) can climb into the 90s (30s Celsius) and higher, and plummet into the 50s (10s Celsius) at night. Afternoon temperatures average in the 60s and 70s (10s–20s Celsius) in spring and fall, and again, evenings are usually cool. Afternoon showers are fairly common fall through spring. Winter days average in the 40s and 50s (5–10s Celsius), and it seldom drops below zero (–17 Celsius), although much of the land above 5,500 feet is buried beneath several feet of snow.

The high country gets up to 20 feet of snow half the year, so visitors should be experienced in winter travel. November through March, it is wise to expect snow and be prepared. Remember, particularly wet winters lead to incredibly stunning and powerful spring waterfalls, especially in Yosemite.

SPECIAL EVENTS IN YOSEMITE

January to February

Chefs' Holidays. Yosemite hosts nationally renowned chefs, who share their culinary secrets with participants. Cost is $149 per person for a five-course dinner. Packages that include accommodations at The Ahwahnee are available. Call © **559/252-5676** for reservations.

February

The Ahwahnee Romance Package. This is an expensive treat for visitors and includes a 2-night stay, plus a candlelight dinner and other romantic extras. Cost is $1,096 plus tax per couple. There is a similar package at **Yosemite Lodge at the Falls** for about $500 per couple. Call © **559/253-5635** for more information.

November to December

Vintners' Holiday. California's finest winemakers hold tastings in The Ahwahnee Great Lounge. Each session concludes with a Vintners' Banquet. The four-course gala event, held in The Ahwahnee Dining Room, pairs four wines with specially selected food. Cost is $149 per person, including gratuities and wine. Two-, three-, and five-night packages are available. Call © **559/ 252-5676** for reservations.

December

The Bracebridge Dinner 🐾🐾. Held on eight evenings from December 15 to the day after Christmas, this event transports diners to 17th-century England, with music, food, and song. The Ahwahnee Dining Room is the setting for the festivities, bedecked with wreaths, banners, and traditional Yuletide decorations. This popular event requires reservations, which are secured by lottery. Applications are available from December 1 to January 15 and are due February 15 for the following year. Prices change from year to year, but expect to pay around $330 per person. Call © **559/252-5676** for more information.

SPECIAL EVENTS IN SEQUOIA & KINGS CANYON

September

Celebrate Sequoias Festival. Kings Canyon National Park hosts this annual event on the first Saturday of September after Labor Day. This all-day event, which takes place in Grant Grove Village, includes walks to lesser-known sequoia groves, living-history presentations, talks about sequoias by botanists, children's activities, and an arts and crafts fair. Call © **559/565-3341** for more information.

December

Trek to the Tree 🐾🐾🐾. Scheduled for the second Sunday in December at 2:30pm, this annual tradition is the main event at Kings Canyon. The Christmas ceremony takes place at the General Grant Tree and includes a solemn and moving tribute to Americans who have given their lives in service to their country. Former Supt. Col. John White said it best: "We are gathered here around a tree that is worthy of representing the spirit of America on Christmas Day. That spirit is best expressed in the plain things of life, the love of the family circle, the simple life of the out-of-doors. The tree is a pillar that is a testimony that things of the spirit transcend those of the flesh." The event is organized by the Sanger Chamber of Commerce (© **559/875-4575**).

3 Passes & Permits You Can Get in Advance

American parks and monuments are some of the biggest travel bargains in the world. If you plan to visit a number of national parks and monuments within a year, a **National Parks Pass,** which costs $50, will save you a bundle. The passes are good at all properties under the jurisdiction of the National Park Service, but not at sites administered by the Bureau of Land Management, National Forest Service, or other federal or state agencies. The National Parks Passes provide free entrance for the pass holder and all vehicle occupants to National Park Service properties that charge vehicle entrance fees, and they also provide free entrance to the pass holder, spouse, parents, and children for those National Park Service Properties that charge per-person fees. The passes can be purchased at park entrance stations and visitor centers, or by mail order (© **888/GO-PARKS;** www.nationalparks.org).

Also available at Park Service properties, as well as other federal recreation sites that charge entrance fees, is the **Golden Age Passport,** for those 62 and older, which has a one-time fee of $10 and provides free admission to all national parks and monuments, plus a 50% discount on camping fees. The **Golden Access Passport,** free for blind or permanently disabled U.S. citizens, has the same benefits as the Golden Age Passport, and is available at all federal recreation sites that charge entrance fees.

Available from U.S Forest Service, Bureau of Land Management, and Fish and Wildlife areas are **Golden Eagle Passes.** For $65 for 1 year from the date of purchase, they allow the bearer, plus everyone traveling with him or her in the same vehicle, free admission to all National Park Service properties, plus free admission to other federal recreation sites that charge fees. The National Parks Pass discussed above can be upgraded to Golden Eagle status for $15. You can purchase the Golden Eagle Pass at sites that honor the pass and at Forest Service offices.

You'll need a **backcountry permit** to camp overnight in the wilderness sections of these parks. (For details, see chapter 3, "Exploring Yosemite," chapter 4, "Hikes & Other Outdoor Pursuits in Yosemite," chapter 6, "Exploring Sequoia & Kings Canyon," and chapter 7, "Hikes & Other Outdoor Pursuits in Sequoia & Kings Canyon.") Permits cost $5 per person in Yosemite and $15 per permit in Sequoia &

Kings Canyon; and it's a good idea to reserve one in advance during the high season. For permits in Yosemite, call © **209/372-0740** or stop by any Wilderness Permit Station. In Sequoia & Kings Canyon, call © **559/565-3341**. Information is also available online at **www. nps.gov/yose** for Yosemite or **www.nps.gov/seki** for Sequoia & Kings Canyon.

Elsewhere in the parks, the usual permits and regulations apply. All anglers over 16 must have valid California fishing licenses.

4 Getting There

YOSEMITE

BY PLANE

Fresno-Yosemite International Airport (© **559/621-4500;** www. flyfresno.org), located 90 miles from the South Entrance at Wawona, is the nearest major airport, serving over 25 cities with more than 100 flights daily. Airlines include Alaska, Allegiant Air, America West/Mesa, American/American Eagle, Continental, Delta, Frontier, Hawaiian, Horizon, Northwest, SkyWest, and United.

Mariposa-Yosemite Airport (© **209/966-2143**) has a tiny airstrip with space for 50 private planes.

BY CAR

Yosemite is a 3½-hour drive from San Francisco and a 6-hour drive from Los Angeles. Many roads lead to Yosemite's four entrances. From the west, the Big Oak Flat Entrance is 88 miles from Manteca via CA 120, which passes through the towns of Groveland, Buck Meadows, and Big Oak Flat. The Arch Rock Entrance is 75 miles northeast of Merced via CA 140, which passes through Mariposa and El Portal. The South Entrance is 64 miles north of Fresno and passes through Oakhurst, Bass Lake, and Fish Camp. From the east, the Tioga Pass Entrance is the only option. It is 10 miles west of Lee Vining via CA 120, although this route is usually open only in the summer. To check on statewide road conditions, call © **800/427-7623** in California or 916/445-7623 outside of the state.

BY BUS

Daily bus transportation into the park from Merced, Mariposa, and other nearby communities is provided by the **Yosemite Area Regional Transportation System (YARTS)** (© **877/989-2787** or 209/388-9589; www.yarts.com). Buses are not subject to park entrance delays during peak season. From Merced, there are several YARTS departures daily from the airport, the Amtrak train station,

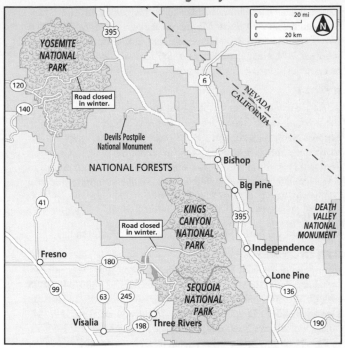

and the Greyhound bus terminal. Round-trip fare is $20 for adults and $14 for children 12 and under and for seniors 65 and older. There are stops in Mariposa at several lodgings and the visitor center, with round-trip rates of $10 for adults and $9 for children 12 and under and for seniors 65 and older.

Greyhound (© 800/231-2222) also links Merced with many other California cities.

BY TRAIN
Amtrak (© 800/872-7245) has routes to Fresno and Merced.

SEQUOIA & KINGS CANYON
BY PLANE
Once again, **Fresno-Yosemite International Airport** (© 559/621-4500; www.flyfresno.org) is the nearest major airport, located 53 miles from the Big Stump Entrance in Kings Canyon, and serving more than 25 cities with more than 100 flights daily. Airlines include Alaska, Allegiant Air, America West/Mesa, American/American Eagle,

Continental, Delta, Frontier, Hawaiian, Horizon, Northwest, Sky-West, and United. **Visalia Municipal Airport** (© 559/713-4201; www.flyvisalia.com), 36 miles from the Ash Mountain Entrance, is served by United Express (© 559/713-4201) with daily flights to LAX.

BY CAR

There are two entrances to the parks—CA 198 east, via Visalia and the town of Three Rivers, leads to the Ash Mountain Entrance in Sequoia National Park, and CA 180 east, via Fresno, leads straight to the Big Stump Entrance near Grant Grove in Kings Canyon National Park. Both entrances are approximately 4 hours from Los Angeles and 5 hours from San Francisco. To check on statewide road conditions, call © 800/427-7623.

BY BUS

Greyhound (© 800/231-2222) serves Visalia and Fresno.

RENTAL CARS

Although not available in either of the parks, most of the major car-rental companies can be found in Fresno: **Avis** (© 800/230-4898 or 559/251-5001); **Budget** (© 800/527-0700 or 559/253-4100); **Dollar** (© 866/434-2226); **Hertz** (© 800/654-3131 or 559/251-5055); and **Alamo/National** (© 800/227-7368 or 559/251-5577).

RVs are another option, although motor homes, especially the larger ones, are a bit difficult to maneuver on the crowded Yosemite Valley roads. **Cruise America** (© 800/RV4RENT; www.cruiseamerica.com) is the country's largest RV-rental company, with outlets in many cities nationwide. RV rentals are also available from **El Monte RV** (© 888/337-2214; www.elmonte.com) and **Road Bear RV** (© 866/491-9853; www.roadbearrv.com). When traveling by RV, however, it's important to call the park ahead of time to check on vehicle length restrictions in campgrounds and even on some of the roadways. Information on additional rental agencies, as well as tips on renting, can be obtained from the **Recreational Vehicle Rental Association,** 3930 University Dr., Fairfax, VA 22030 (www.rvra.org).

5 Learning & Adventure Vacations

The nonprofit **Yosemite Association** (© 209/379-2321 or 209/379-2646; www.yosemite.org) offers more than 60 **"Outdoor Adventures"** ⨍ covering subjects from backpacking, to natural history, to photography. Most of the programs are multiday, with charges of about $80 per day per person (not including lodging and meals), and often include hikes or backpacking trips.

Sequoia Field Institute ✯, HCR 89, Box 10, Three Rivers, CA 93271 (© **559/565-4251;** http://www.sequoiahistory.org/sfi/sfi.htm), offers a number of field seminars in and around Sequoia & Kings Canyon National Parks. The programs typically run from 1 to 4 days, with fees ranging from $75 for the 1-day seminars to $100 and up for the multiday programs. Topics vary, but are likely to include subjects such as mountain wildflowers, black bears, photography, and, of course, giant sequoias. Some seminars have minimum age limits, and some are physically demanding.

Daylong van tours of Sequoia are available through **Sequoia Sightseeing Tours** (© **559/561-4189;** www.sequoiatours.com) for $72 for each adult and half that for kids 12 and under.

6 Tips for Travelers with Disabilities

People visit these parks to witness their beauty, and that can be done in a host of different ways—you don't have to hike 5 miles or climb to the top of a waterfall. Some of the most rewarding moments come from quiet, still observation.

Be sure to inquire about the National Park Service's free **Golden Access Pass,** available to the blind and permanently disabled. See "Passes & Permits You Can Get in Advance," above.

In Yosemite, there are some fairly level paved trails around the valley floor, including the ones to Mirror Lake and Happy Isles, and the paved bike trail (see "Bicycling," in chapter 4) is also accessible to wheelchairs. Ask for information on accessible points when making reservations. An accessibility brochure is available at park entrances and visitor centers, and wheelchairs can be rented at the **Yosemite Medical Clinic** (© **209/372-4637**) and the **Yosemite Lodge Bike Rental Stand** (© **209/372-1208**).

In Sequoia & Kings Canyon, the visitor centers in the Foothills, Lodgepole, and Grant Grove are wheelchair accessible. Paved trails lead to the General Sherman Tree and General Grant Tree. In Giant Forest, there are a few paved trails (including Big Trees Trail). There are modified picnic tables at Hospital Rock and Big Stump. Special requests should be directed to © **559/565-3134.**

Wheelchair Getaways (© **800/642-2042** or 859/873-4973; www.wheelchair-getaways.com) rents specialized vans with wheelchair lifts and other features for the disabled, with outlets in most Western states.

7 Tips for Travelers with Pets

Pets are not particularly welcome at national parks. In Yosemite, pets are not allowed on unpaved trails or in buildings; they must be leashed at all times and may never be left alone. Pets are permitted in all campgrounds except Camp 4 Walk-In, Tamarack Flat, and Porcupine Flat. There's a dog **kennel** (© **209/372-8348**), open daily 7:30am to 5pm in the summer, at the stable in Yosemite Valley. Dogs must be at least 16 weeks old, weigh over 20 pounds, and have a license and proof of current shots. The fee is $8 per day.

Sequoia & Kings Canyon has similar regulations. Pets are allowed in all campgrounds but not on any trails or in the backcountry. A good rule of thumb issued by the Park Service: You can take your pet wherever you can take your car, but keep it on a leash.

8 Tips for Travelers with Children

Yosemite schedules a number of children's programs. Kids ages 3 to 6 can join the Little Cubs, and those from 7 to 13 can become Junior Rangers, by completing projects in a booklet ($3 for Little Cubs and $3.50 for Junior Rangers); those in the Junior Ranger program also collect a bag of trash and participate in a ranger program. Upon completion, Little Cubs receive a button; Junior Rangers receive a patch. The booklets are available at the Nature Center at Happy Isles, Yosemite Valley and Tuolumne Meadows visitor centers, and the Wawona and Big Oak Flat information stations.

Free ranger-led walks and talks are held at various locations throughout the park, and many are suitable for kids. The programs vary by season, so check your *Yosemite Today* (handed out at park entrances) to find out what's happening during your visit. The Indian Cultural Museum (shuttle bus stops nos. 5 and 9) has exhibits and brief lectures conducted by descendants of Yosemite's first residents. The Happy Isles Nature Center (shuttle bus stop no. 16) has displays and dioramas of park animals that children will enjoy.

During the summer Sequoia & Kings Canyon offers ranger-led walks aimed at kids and families, and a campfire program at Lodgepole (check at visitor centers for the current schedule). In addition, the parks have a Junior Ranger Program, in which children get booklets and complete various activities to become Junior Rangers. Another child-friendly option is the Beetle Rock Education Center near the Giant Forest Museum, open on summer weekends only.

Tips **The Bear Necessities**

Bears have broken into thousands of cars in Yosemite National Park. If you'd like your vehicle left intact during your visit, never leave food inside your car; use the storage facilities in the park.

9 Protecting Your Health & Safety

Common sense should be your guiding rule when visiting these parks, but here are some of the basics:

- Although some of the bridges that cross rivers and streams look inviting, resist the temptation to use them as diving boards—it's not only dangerous, it's illegal.
- Trails, especially ones over rock and granite, can be slick. Be especially careful along any rivers or creeks, such as Mist Trail in Yosemite, where wind and water can make for treacherous conditions.
- Always carry more than enough water, especially when going into higher elevations where our bodies require more hydration.
- Under no circumstances should food be left in tents, cabins, or cars. There are storage lockers and bear-proof containers throughout the park—use them.
- Under no circumstances should you feed a bear—or any wild animal, for that matter.
- Always carry a map if you go hiking, even for short day hikes.

10 Protecting the Environment

These parks are incredibly beautiful and a joy to experience, and it is our responsibility as park visitors to keep them that way. Don't feed the animals. Don't litter. Don't take anything home that you didn't buy or bring with you. Share trails and walkways, and stay on them. If this sounds like something you learned in grade school, it is, but sometimes people need a gentle reminder that 50 million years of work deserves respect.

It's relatively easy to be a good outdoor citizen—mostly common sense. Pack out all trash, stay on established trails, be careful not to pollute water, and do your best to have as little impact on the environment as possible. Some hikers go further, carrying a small trash bag to pick up litter. As the park service likes to remind us, protecting our national parks is everyone's responsibility.

3

Exploring Yosemite

Yosemite's towering geologic formations, lush meadows, tumbling rivers, and spectacular waterfalls attract travelers from around the world. Yosemite is home to 3 of the world's 10 tallest waterfalls and the largest single piece of exposed granite on the planet. It boasts some of the world's largest trees and what is possibly the world's most recognized rock formation. And you don't have to be a mountaineer to enjoy the beauty of the park—Yosemite's most popular attractions are accessible to everyone, whether you want to hike around or just stand and stare. No matter where you go, you'll find a view worth remembering.

1 Essentials

ACCESS/ENTRY POINTS

There are four entrances to Yosemite: the Big Oak Flat Entrance and the Arch Rock Entrance from the west, the South Entrance, and the Tioga Pass Entrance from the east. Make sure to get a copy of the biweekly *Yosemite Today* when you come in for up-to-date information on ranger programs and other park events and activities.

VISITOR CENTERS & INFORMATION

In the park, the biggest visitor center is the **Valley Visitor Center** in Yosemite Village (© **209/372-0200**), which provides all sorts of information, offers daily ranger programs, and is conveniently located near restaurants and shopping. You can talk with park rangers about your plans for exploring the park, and bulletin boards display information on current road conditions and campsite availability, and also serve as a message board for visitors. There are several exhibits on the park, its geologic history, and the history of the valley. This center provides information on bears and also has information on the impact that humans have on the park. A shop sells maps, books, videos, postcards, posters, and the like. Nearby is the **Yosemite Valley Wilderness Center,** with high-country maps, information on necessary hiking and camping equipment, trail information, and a ranger on hand to answer questions, issue permits, and offer advice about the high country. Information is also available at the **Wawona Information Station** and the **Big Oak Flat Information Center.** In the high country, stop in at the **Tuolumne Meadows Visitor Center** (𝒞 **209/372-0263,** although it's always best to call 209/372-0200 in summer). Questions about visitor-related services, including tours and accommodations, can be answered at 𝒞 **209/372-1000.**

FEES

It costs $20 per car per week to enter the valley, or $10 per person per week if arriving on bicycle, on motorcycle, or on foot. The Yosemite Pass, for $40, covers entry into the park for a year.

It costs $5 to $18 a night to camp in a Yosemite campground (𝒞 **800/436-7275;** http://reservations.nps.gov). It's best to book at least 5 months in advance if you are planning to camp during the summer, especially in Yosemite Valley. It's worth checking back if you missed out because cancellations do occur. Reservations are accepted up to 5 months in advance, beginning on the 15th of each month. For example, a camper wanting a reservation for August 1 can apply no earlier than March 15. Additional campground information is available by phone (𝒞 **209/372-0200**) or online (www. nps.gov/yose/trip/camping.htm).

REGULATIONS

The regulations here are similar to those at most other National Park Service properties—don't damage the resources, no pets or bikes on trails, observe campground quiet hours, and the like—but here the storage of food, or anything that bears might think counts as food, is also strictly regulated. In many cases, you'll need to place food and items that smell like they might be food (perfume and even toothpaste) in bear-proof canisters or lockers. Regulations are posted throughout the park, and you'll also receive information when you enter the park, but we strongly suggest that you carry as little food, cosmetics, and so on as possible.

FAST FACTS: Yosemite National Park

ATMs You'll find automatic teller machines in the Village Store, just south of the Village Store, in the main registration area at Yosemite Lodge, inside the grocery store at Curry Village, in the

Wawona Store, and at Yosemite View Lodge on CA 140 in El Portal.

Car Trouble/Towing Services Call the Village Garage (© 209/372-8320), which offers 24-hour towing.

Climate See "When to Go," in chapter 2.

Emergencies Call © 911.

Gas Stations There are three gas stations in Yosemite: in the town of Wawona, at Crane Flat, and at Tuolumne Meadows (during the summer only). Travelers with a credit or debit card can purchase gasoline 24 hours a day.

Laundromats There's a laundromat at Housekeeping Camp, which is close to Curry Village in Yosemite Valley.

Maps The best maps of Yosemite are published by the Yosemite Association and sell for $2.50 or $2.95 at just about every sales outlet in the park. Each map covers a specific region—the valley, Wawona, Tuolumne—and includes all pertinent information, including parking, hiking trails, elevations, accommodations, ranger stations, the natural history of each region, and restrooms.

Medical/Dental Clinics There are medical and dental clinics in the valley, near Yosemite Village. The Yosemite Medical Clinic can be reached at © 209/372-4637. The dental clinic is at © 209/372-4200.

Permits Permits are required for all overnight camping in the backcountry (see chapter 4, "Hikes & Other Outdoor Pursuits in Yosemite"). In Yosemite, call © 209/372-0740, or stop by any Wilderness Permit Station or the Valley Wilderness Center.

Post Offices There are post offices in Yosemite Village, Yosemite Lodge, Wawona, Tuolumne Meadows, Curry Village, and El Portal.

Supplies The best selection of supplies in Yosemite is at the Village Store. You can also try the market at Yosemite Lodge, or what are called "camp stores" in Curry Village, Wawona, and Tuolumne Meadows.

Weather Updates for Yosemite are available by phone at © 209/372-0200, or online at www.nps.gov/yose.

2 Orientation

All four main entrances to the park meet in Yosemite Valley, the most popular of the park's three destination points (the other two being Tuolumne Meadows and Wawona). The valley is a mile wide and 7 miles long, set at about 4,000 feet above sea level. The granite walls of Half Dome, El Capitan, and Glacier Point tower another 4,000 feet overhead. The picturesque Merced River, fed by several small brooks and creeks, winds lazily through the length of Yosemite Valley.

It's relatively easy to find your way around Yosemite. All road signs are clear and visible. At first, Yosemite Valley might seem to be a confusing series of roadways, but you'll soon realize that all roads lead to a one-way loop that hugs the valley's perimeter. It is easy to find yourself heading in the wrong direction, so be alert whenever you merge and just follow the signs.

We recommend visitors use year-round shuttle-bus service in the Yosemite Valley; Wawona and Tuolumne Meadows offer a similar service during the summer months only. Driving in any of these places during peak season—or even off-season in the valley—is not fun, so use the shuttles as much as possible.

YOSEMITE VALLEY

Most people come to Yosemite to see this giant study in shadow and light. In spring, after the winter snow begins melting in the high country, waterfalls encircle Yosemite Valley, shimmering like a diamond necklace. There are wide, beautiful meadows, towering trees, and the ever-present sound of rushing water in the background. The great irony is that the original park boundaries, established in 1890, excluded the valley. In addition to the natural phenomena found throughout the valley, there are a number of historical attractions worth exploring as well.

Yosemite Valley contains three developed areas: **Yosemite Village, Yosemite Lodge,** and **Curry Village.** Except for the Ahwahnee Hotel—which is about midway between Yosemite and Curry villages—all the hotels, restaurants, and shops can be found in these areas. Curry Village (also called Camp Curry) and Yosemite Lodge offer the bulk of the park's overnight accommodations. Curry Village is near shuttle-bus stops nos. 13A, 13B, 14, 15, 20, and 21. Yosemite Lodge is served by stop no. 8. Both locations have restaurants and a small grocery. The lodge has a large public swimming pool, and Curry Village has an ice rink open in winter.

Yosemite Valley

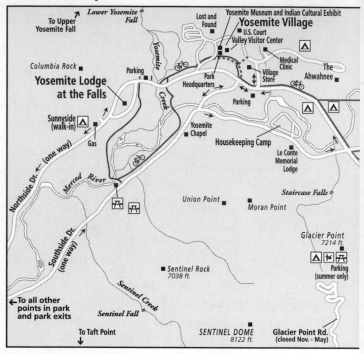

Yosemite Village is the largest developed region within the valley and is served by shuttle-bus stops nos. 1, 2, 4, 5, 9, and 10. It is home to the park's largest visitor center and the headquarters for the National Park Service in Yosemite. The village also has a host of shops and services, including a grocery, restaurants, the valley's only medical clinic, a dentist, a post office, a beauty shop, and an ATM.

Check out the **Yosemite Pioneer Cemetery,** a peaceful graveyard in the shade of tall sequoias, with headstones dating back to the 1800s. There are about 36 marked graves, identifiable by horizontal slabs of rock, some etched with crude or faded writing. There are some Yosemite history notables buried here, such as James Lamon, an early settler who was known for his apple trees—they still bear fruit—and who died in 1875. Pick up the self-guiding booklet at the visitor center.

Next door, you'll find the **Yosemite Museum** and the **Indian Cultural Exhibit.** Both attractions are free and provide a historic

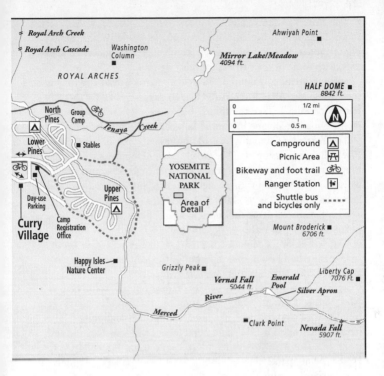

picture of the park, before and after it was settled and secured as a national treasure. The museum entrance is marked by a crowd-pleaser: the cross section of a 1,000-year-old sequoia with memorable dates identified on the tree's rings. The tree section was cut in 1919 from a tree that fell in the Mariposa Grove south of the valley in Wawona. The Indian Cultural Exhibit strives to explain the life of the American Indians who once lived here, and members of regional tribes regularly speak or give demonstrations of traditional arts such as basket weaving. The Yosemite Museum Book Shop is next door and sells books and traditional Indian arts and crafts.

The village of the **Ahwahneeche** (a reproduction of a real Ahwahneeche village) is behind the museum and the Indian Cultural Exhibit. The village offers a free self-guided walking tour accessible from the back door of the visitor center. This exhibit guides visitors through the transformations of the Ahwahneeche, the tribe that inhabited Yosemite Valley until the mid-1850s. The village includes a ceremonial roundhouse that's still in use.

The **Ansel Adams Gallery** (© **209/372-4413;** www.ansel adams.com) sells prints and cards of images made by this famed photographer. The shop also serves as a small gallery for current artisans, with some of their works for sale.

Just a mile east of Yosemite Village on a narrow, dead-end road is the majestic old **Ahwahnee Hotel** (see chapter 5, "Where to Stay & Eat in Yosemite"). Take the shuttle bus to stop no. 3. It's definitely worth a visit for anyone interested in architecture and design.

The **Yosemite Chapel** is located on the south side of the Merced River, shuttle-bus stop no. 11. From the bus stop, walk across the bridge and to the left for just under a quarter mile. Schedules for the worship services held in the chapel are posted in *Yosemite Today* and are available by phone (© **209/372-4831**).

The **LeConte Memorial Lodge** is an educational center and library at shuttle-bus stop no. 12. Built in 1903, in honor of a University of California geologist named Joseph LeConte, the Tudor-style granite building hosts a number of free educational programs and talks, which are listed in *Yosemite Today.*

Beyond Curry Village at the valley's far eastern end is the **Happy Isles Nature Center,** shuttle-bus stop no. 16. Summer hours are from 9am to 5pm daily; it is closed spring, fall, and winter. The nature center offers exhibits and books about the varied animal and plant life found in Yosemite; it's a super place for children to explore. The park's Little Cub and Junior Ranger programs, described in "Tips for Travelers with Children" in chapter 2, are held here as well. Happy Isles is named for three nearby inlets labeled by Yosemite's guardian in 1880.

NORTH OF THE VALLEY

Hetch Hetchy and **Tuolumne Meadows** are remarkably different regions located on opposite sides of the park. Hetch Hetchy is on the park's western border and can be reached by taking the turnoff just outside the park's Big Oak Flat Entrance. Tuolumne Meadows

---

Moments **Alpenglow**

You're in for a real treat if you position yourself with a view of the mountains and granite outcroppings around sunrise or sunset. The light of the rising and setting sun casts a rich, brilliant pink glow (known as alpenglow) on the landscape. This is a terrific time for photographing the area.

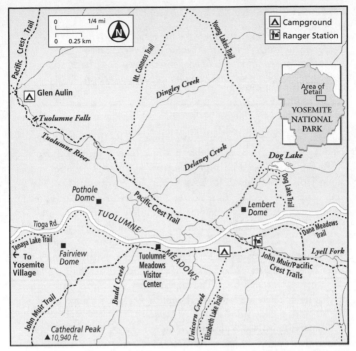

is on the park's eastern border, just inside Tioga Pass, and is inaccessible by motor vehicle during the winter. (Tioga Rd. is the road that leads to the meadows.)

Hetch Hetchy is home to the park's reservoir, passionately opposed by the famed conservationist John Muir and reviled by environmentalists to this day. Many believe that losing the battle over the reservoir exhausted Muir and hastened his death. Muir passed away in 1914, a year after the bill was signed to fund the dam project. Construction began on the dam in 1919, and it was completed in 1923. The reservoir provides San Francisco with drinking water; the dam generates a bit of electricity for the city as well.

South of Hetch Hetchy are two large stands of giant sequoias. The Merced and Tuolumne groves offer a quiet alternative to the Mariposa Grove of Big Trees in Wawona. Both groves are accessible only on foot. The Merced Grove is a 4-mile round-trip walk that begins about 4½ miles inside the Big Oak Flat Entrance. Although the trees here don't mirror the majesty of the Mariposa Grove, the

---

Impressions

The big Tuolumne Meadows are flowery lawns, lying along the south fork of the Tuolumne River . . . here the mountains seem to have been cleared away or sit back, so that wide-open views may be had in every direction.

—John Muir

---

solitude here makes this a real treat for hikers. The Tuolumne Grove (about 25 trees) can be reached by a 1-mile hike (2 hr. round-trip).

To get into Yosemite's **high country,** go about 1½ hours east along Tioga Road, which is closed in winter between Big Oak Flat and Tioga Pass. (You'll need skis or snowshoes to access this area during the winter.) This subalpine region is low on amenities, making it the frequent haunt of those who enjoy roughing it, but even cushy-soft couch potatoes can enjoy the beauty up here. Glistening granite domes tower above lush green meadows, which are cut by silver swaths of streams and lakes. Many of Yosemite's longer hikes begin or pass through here. The high country is explored at length in chapter 4. There are some worthwhile sights here for anyone willing to venture away from the valley masses.

Olmsted Point ⟨⟨⟨, located midway between White Wolf and Tuolumne Meadows, offers one of the most spectacular vistas anywhere in the park. Here the enormous walls of the Tenaya Canyon are exposed and an endless view stretches all the way to Yosemite Valley. In the distance are Cloud's Rest and the rear of Half Dome. To the east, Tenaya Lake, one of the park's larger lakes (and an easily accessible one), glistens like a sapphire.

About 8 miles east of Tenaya Lake is **Tuolumne Meadows,** a huge subalpine area surrounded by domes and steep granite formations that offer exhilarating climbs. The meadow is a beautiful place to hike and fish, or just to admire the scenery while escaping the crowds of Yosemite Valley. Facing to the north of the meadow is Lembert Dome at about two o'clock, and then working clockwise, Johnson Peak at seven o'clock, Unicorn Peak at eight o'clock, Fairview Dome at ten o'clock, and Pothole Dome at eleven o'clock. Up the road is the central region of Tuolumne, where you'll find a visitor center, campground, canvas tent-cabins, and a store. Continue east to reach Tioga Lake and Tioga Pass.

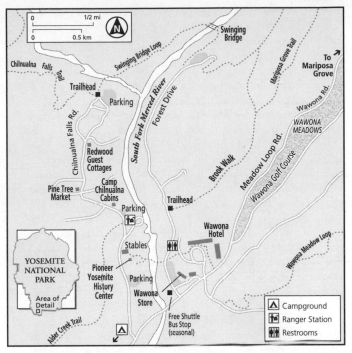

SOUTH OF THE VALLEY

This region, which includes Wawona and the Mariposa Grove of Big Trees, is densely forested. A handful of granite rock formations dot the area, but they are nothing like those found elsewhere. En route to Wawona from the valley, you'll come across several wonderful views of Yosemite Valley. Tunnel View, a turnout just before passing through a long tunnel along Wawona Road, provides one of the park's most recognizable vistas, memorialized on film by photographer Ansel Adams. To the right is Bridalveil Fall, opposite El Capitan. Half Dome lies straight ahead.

Halfway between Yosemite Valley and Wawona is Glacier Point Road (closed in winter past the turnoff to Badger Pass Ski Area), which runs 16 miles to spectacular **Glacier Point** ✸✸✸. From the parking area, it's a short hike to an amazing overlook that provides a view of the glacier-carved granite rock formations all along the valley and beyond. At this point you will be at eye level with Half Dome, which looks close enough to reach out and touch. Far below,

Yosemite Valley resembles a green-carpeted ant farm. There are also some pretty sights of obscure waterfalls that are not visible from the valley floor. Glacier Point has a geology hut and a day lodge for wintertime cross-country skiers. The day lodge morphs into a gift store/snack shack during the rest of the year. Glacier Point and the lodge are accessible both by foot and bus (see "Organized Tours & Ranger Programs," later in this chapter).

Continue south on Wawona Road to reach **Wawona,** a small town that runs deep with history, located 30 miles from the valley. It was settled in 1856 by homesteader Galen Clark, who built a rustic way station for travelers en route from Mariposa to Yosemite. The property's next owners, the Washburn brothers, built much of what is today the Wawona Hotel, including the large white building to the right of the main hotel, which was constructed in 1876. The two-story hotel annex went up 3 years later. When Congress established Yosemite National Park in 1890 and charged the U.S. Army with managing it, Wawona was chosen as the Army's headquarters. For 16 summers, the cavalry out of San Francisco occupied the camp and mapped the park. When Yosemite Valley was added to the park after the turn of the century, the cavalry picked up and relocated to the valley.

Near the Wawona Hotel are Hill's Studio and the Pioneer Yosemite History Center. The studio keeps sporadic hours that are hard to pin down but listed in *Yosemite Today,* and is the former workspace of noted 19th-century painter Thomas Hill. Hill painted a number of award-winning landscapes, including some recognizable ones of Yosemite.

The Pioneer Center offers a self-guided walking tour of cabins and buildings that were moved to this site in 1961 from various locations in the park. Each building represents a different period in Yosemite's short history. During the summer, National Park Service interpreters dress in period clothing and act out characters from the park's past. To reach the center, walk across the covered bridge. An entertaining 10-minute stagecoach ride is offered during the summer for a small fee.

Nearby, the **Mariposa Grove** is a stand of giant sequoias, some of which have been around for 3,000 years. They stretch almost 300 feet tall, are 50 feet in circumference, and weigh an average of 2 million pounds. The 500 trees here are divided into the Upper Grove and the Lower Grove. The easiest way to see the trees is from the open-air **tram** (© **209/375-1621** for reservations) that runs during summer. Cost is $16 for adults and $10 for children; kids under 5

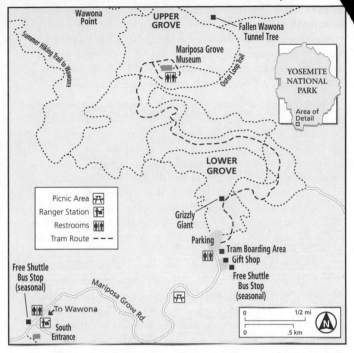

ride free. Trams leave from the Mariposa Grove parking area every 20 minutes. A guide provides commentary during the trip, which lasts about an hour. The tram makes regular stops at the Grizzly Giant, Wawona Tunnel Tree, and Mariposa Grove Museum. It's worth hopping out and walking around as often as possible. Just take the next tram back. All of the area is also accessible on foot. It is an uphill walk to the upper grove, 2.5 miles each way.

The Grizzly Giant is the largest tree in the grove. At "just" 200 feet, it is shorter than some of its neighbors, but its trunk measures more than 30 feet in diameter at the base. A huge limb halfway up the tree measures 6 feet in diameter and is bigger than many of the "young" trees in the grove.

The Wawona Tunnel Tree had a tunnel 10 feet high and 26 feet long cut through it in 1881. Thousands of visitors were photographed driving through the tree before it toppled in the winter of 1968–69, its death finally caused by heavy snow. No one saw the tree fall. Another tunnel tree, the California Tree, had a tunnel cut

d still stands near the Grizzly Giant, beckoning visitors
through it.

The Mariposa Grove Museum resides in Galen Clark's first building. It was last refurbished in 1981 and is usually open from late
spring into the fall, featuring various exhibits. Books and educational materials are also sold here from late spring into fall.

3 The Highlights

Spectacular **Yosemite Falls** 🐾🐾🐾 is a three-part waterfall that
stretches 2,425 feet skyward, making it one of the tallest waterfalls
in the world. In spring, snow runoff makes it a magnificent specta-
cle as spray crashes to the base of the falls, leaving visitors drenched.
In the winter, cold temperatures help form a cone at the base of the
waterfall, sometimes reaching 200 feet high—it looks like a giant
upside-down snow cone. You can reach the base of Yosemite Falls by
taking the shuttle bus to stop no. 6. It is also an easy walk from any
parking lot near Yosemite Lodge.

Picturesque **Mirror Lake** 🐾, named for its nearly perfect reflec-
tion of the surrounding scenery, is slowly filling with sediments, and
depending on the spring runoff, may be little more than a watering
hole by late summer. Still, the lake captures beautiful images of Half
Dome and North Dome, which tower above. It is surrounded by
forest and has a fairly level, paved trail along its banks, which also
offer places to sunbathe and picnic. It's accessible (by vehicle) to
people with disabilities; there's a 60-foot elevation gain. Take the
shuttle to stop no. 17.

The **Mist Trail** to Vernal Fall shows the power behind the water that
flows through Yosemite. The trail itself can be slick and treacherous,
but it is a pretty walk up 500 steps to the top of the waterfall (see chapter 4). Miniature rainbows dot the trail as mist from the waterfall
splashes below and ricochets back onto the trail. This walk is sometimes closed in winter due to ice, but there is a winter route to the top
of the fall. (For the winter route, see the hike descriptions in chapter 4.)

The remnants of a recent rockslide can be seen behind the Happy
Isles Nature Center. Several years ago, a granite slab collapsed with
such force that it blew over hundreds of trees, claimed one life, and
filled the valley with dust. Park officials decided to leave the landscape pretty much as it was post-slide, as a reminder of the tremendous geologic forces that shaped (and are still shaping) the park.

The **view from Glacier Point** 🐾🐾🐾 is one of the most spectacular vistas in the park. From this point, far above the valley floor,

visitors will find themselves at eye level with Half Dome and hundreds of feet above most of the park's waterfalls. The white and silver rocks offer a stark contrast against the sky. To reach Glacier Point in summer, take one of the buses (check at tour desks for information) or drive south of the valley on Wawona Road to the turnoff for Glacier Point Road. Follow the winding road to the parking lot (allow about 45 min. from the valley) and walk a few hundred yards to the lookout. In winter, the road is closed and Glacier Point is accessible only on skis or snowshoes.

A **drive toward the high country** on Tioga Road offers other breathtaking views. To our thinking, some of the grandest sights are at **Olmsted Point** *☆☆*, which provides a panoramic view of the granite landscape. There are nearby picnic spots at picturesque Tenaya Lake. A bit farther is the emerald-green Tuolumne Meadows, which is dotted with thousands of wildflowers during late spring and summer (see "Exploring the Backcountry," in chapter 4).

An **off-season visit** to Yosemite Valley, especially in winter, offers unique beauty plus the peace and quiet that was once commonplace in Yosemite. And although the high country is inaccessible by car—Tioga Pass Road and Glacier Point Road are usually closed to vehicles from mid-fall to early June, depending on snowfall—the valley becomes more accessible, as the number of visitors is greatly reduced. Snow dusts the granite peaks and valley floor, bends trees, and creates a winter wonderland for visitors. Lodging rates drop, and it is slightly easier to secure accommodations or a campground site, but even a day trip can be rewarding. Even though many animals hibernate during the cold months, this is the best time of year to see the valley as it was before it became such a popular place.

4 How to See the Park in 1 or 2 Days

This is a park that begs for an extended visit, but those with a limited amount of time will also have an enjoyable experience, especially if they make use of the park's shuttle bus. The bus is free, easy to use, and operates year-round, with fewer stops in winter. For that reason, we've included shuttle-bus stop numbers wherever possible throughout the valley sections in this book. Bus stops are well marked and within easy walking distance of all parking lots.

You can get on and off the shuttles at any point, but be sure to stop in the Valley Visitor Center (shuttle-bus stops nos. 5 and 9) for an orientation on the forces that carved the valley.

If you're not interested in taking off and exploring alone, take one of the guided tours (see "Organized Tours & Ranger Programs," below).

The base of **Lower Yosemite Fall** (shuttle-bus stop no. 6) is an easy walk from either Yosemite Village or Yosemite Lodge. From the base, you can see a portion of the magnificent water show. During peak runoff, it's not uncommon to get wet, as the force of the fall sends spray in every direction. In late winter and early spring, a huge snow cone caused by freezing water rises up to 200 feet from the base of this fall. The hike up the fall is described in detail in chapter 4.

Happy Isles (shuttle-bus stop no. 16) is another major attraction. Located at the convergence of several inlets, the valley's nature center is an especially great stop for those traveling with kids, but the area gets most of its traffic because it is also the trailhead for Vernal and Nevada falls, two picturesque staircase waterfalls that can only be reached by foot. Both hikes are described in chapter 4.

Next, we recommend a visit to **Mirror Lake** (shuttle-bus stop no. 17), a small lake named for the near-perfect way it reflects the surrounding scenery. It's slowly filling up with silt and is less dramatic and mirror-like than it used to be, but its shore still offers a beautiful view of Half Dome. This short stroll is well marked and described in chapter 4.

If you still have more time to explore, choose anything that piques your interest from a variety of hikes and activities. To make the most of your time, stick with the recommendations we list throughout the following chapters.

5 Seeing the Park by Car & Shuttle

In the eastern section of Yosemite Valley, two words pertain—*shuttle bus*. The only reasons to use your private vehicle are to enter and to exit.

Elsewhere in the park, however, a vehicle is more appropriate. If you want to explore Wawona or Tuolumne, hike near Tenaya Lake, or check out Mariposa Grove, having your car is convenient because there is currently no direct bus service from the valley to these destinations. Some sample package tours that allow you to leave the driving to others are described below, or you can inquire at tour desks in Yosemite Village, The Ahwahnee, Yosemite Lodge, and Curry Village. So unless the Park Service develops a transportation

---

> *Tips* **Taking Aim at Traffic**
>
> In an attempt to reduce the traffic volume at Yosemite National Park, a new park bus system began operating in the summer of 2000. An estimated 7,000 cars enter Yosemite on any given day, leaving many visitors mired in traffic jams. The project, a joint effort between the National Park Service and the Yosemite Area Regional Transportation System (YARTS), shuttles visitors into Yosemite from nearby communities and commuter lots along the three highways leading into the park. Although it is still a bit early to claim success, park officials are optimistic about the project's ability to help manage Yosemite's traffic problems, thereby providing all Yosemite visitors with a better and more satisfying experience.

---

system that reaches beyond the valley walls, automobile travel will remain necessary.

6 Organized Tours & Ranger Programs

The park offers a number of **ranger-guided walks, hikes, and other programs.** Check at one of the visitor centers or in *Yosemite Today* for current topics, start times, and locations. Walks may vary from week to week, but you can always count on nature hikes, evening discussions on park anomalies (floods, fires, or critters), and the sunrise photography program aimed at replicating some of Ansel Adams's works. The sunrise photo walk always gets rave reviews from the early risers who venture out at dawn. All photo walks require advance registration. (Get details at the visitor centers.) The living-history evening program outside at Yosemite Lodge is great for young and old alike.

Several organizations also host guided trips. **Yosemite Guides** *&&* (© 877/425-3366; www.yosemiteguides.com) offers guided trips to some of the lesser-known areas of the park and also guides fly-fishing trips for all levels. The **Yosemite Institute** *&&* (© 209/379-9511; www.yni.org) is a nonprofit organization offering elementary and middle-school students a unique environment for learning about nature and the human history of the Sierra Nevada. Also check out **Incredible Adventures** (© 800/777-8464; www.incadventures.com), which offers 3-day trips and hikes in Yosemite from San Francisco.

Yosemite Sightseeing Tours *&* (© 559/658-8687; www.yosemite tours.com) conducts scheduled tours as well as customized trips.

Costs run about $80 for adults, $40 for kids. Tours are operated on small air-conditioned buses with huge picture windows. The sightseeing includes Mariposa Grove, Yosemite Valley, and Glacier Point. Geology, flora, and fauna are pointed out along the way. Stops are scheduled for lunch, shopping, and photo opportunities. Pickup can be arranged from various motels throughout Oakhurst and Bass Lake.

A variety of **guided bus tours** are also available. You can buy tickets at tour desks at Yosemite Lodge, The Ahwahnee, Curry Village, or beside the Village Store in Yosemite Village. Advance reservations are suggested for all tours, and space can be reserved in person or by phone (© **209/372-1240**). Always double-check at tour desks for updated departure schedules and prices. Most tours depart from Yosemite Lodge, The Ahwahnee, or Curry Village, and prices range from about $22 for adults for a 2-hour tour, to about $60 for adults for full-day trips. Children's rates are usually half that, and discounts are offered for seniors.

The 2-hour **Valley Floor Tour** is a great way to get acclimated to the park, providing a good selection of photo ops, including El Capitan, Tunnel View, and Half Dome. This ride is also available on nights when the moon is full or near full. It's an eerie but beautiful scene when moonlight illuminates the valley's granite walls and gives visitors a rare picture of Yosemite. Blankets and hot cocoa are provided. Dress warmly, though, because it can get mighty chilly after the sun goes down.

The **Glacier Point Tour** is a 4-hour scenic bus ride through the valley to Glacier Point. Tours also depart from Yosemite Valley to **Tuolumne Meadows.** The Mariposa Grove trip takes 8 hours, and is especially popular with hikers who want to explore the high country without relocating their camp from the valley floor.

If you're staying in the valley, the **National Park Service** and **DNC Parks & Resorts at Yosemite** present evening programs on the park's history and culture. Past summer programs have included discussions on early expeditions to Yosemite, the park's flora and fauna, geology, global ecology, and the legends of the American Indians who once lived here. Other programs have focused on Mark Wellman's courageous climb of El Capitan—he made the ascent as a paraplegic—and major threats to Yosemite's environment.

Inquire about current programs upon check-in at your hotel or at the information booth outside the visitor center. Although most programs are held in the valley, a few campgrounds offer campfire programs in the summer.

Spring through fall, the **Yosemite Theater** offers inexpensive theatrical and musical programs designed to supplement Park Service programs. They tend to repeat from year to year, but old favorites include a conversation with John Muir, a film on Yosemite's future, and singalongs.

4

Hikes & Other Outdoor Pursuits in Yosemite

A nature lover's paradise, Yosemite has some of the most beautiful scenery you'll see anywhere, and the best way to experience the park is to get out onto the trails. Park rangers lead walks and hikes (see "Organized Tours & Ranger Programs," in chapter 3), and guided day treks are also available from **Yosemite Guides** (© **877/425-3366** or 209/379-2231), with rates from $60 to $70 per person.

1 Day Hikes & Scenic Walks

Below is a selection of day hikes throughout Yosemite National Park. Distances and times are round-trip estimates unless otherwise noted.

IN & NEAR THE VALLEY

Base of Bridalveil Fall Bridalveil Fall measures 620 feet from top to bottom. In the spring, expect to get wet. This walk is wheelchair accessible with strong assistance. It's a beautiful waterfall, and easy access makes it a favorite.

0.5 miles/30 min. Easy. Drive or walk to the Bridalveil Fall parking area, about 3 miles west of Yosemite Village. Follow trail markers.

Columbia Rock This hike mirrors the initial ascent of the Upper Yosemite Fall trail (see below), but stops at Columbia Rock, 1,000 feet above the valley. You won't find a valley view, but the sights here are still impressive. The trail is also less likely to get an accumulation of snow because it's on the sunny side of the valley.

2 miles/2–3 hr. Moderate. Use the trail head for Upper Yosemite Fall (see below).

Four-Mile Trail to Glacier Point This trail climbs 3,200 feet, but efforts will be rewarded with terrific views of Yosemite Valley's north rim. Check on trail conditions before setting out; it's usually closed in winter. The trail ends at Glacier Point, but if you'd like to extend the hike, you can connect there to the Panorama Trail (see below), but beware: The combined round-trip distance is 14 miles.

9.6 miles/7–10 hr. Strenuous. The trail head is 1.25 miles from Yosemite Village, at the Four Mile parking area at the marker post "V-18," or take the shuttle bus to the Yosemite Lodge, stop 8, and walk behind the Lodge over the Swinging Bridge to Southeast Dr. The trail head is 0.25 miles west.

Half Dome   This long, steep trip, which about 1,000 hikers do each summer day, climbs 4,900 feet. From Happy Isles, take the Mist Trail or the John Muir Trail past Vernal and Nevada falls, and up and into Little Yosemite Valley. Leave the John Muir Trail for the Half Dome Trail. Hiking the final 600 feet up the back of Half Dome requires the use of cables installed in the rock, and a strong heart is helpful, too. Half Dome has a small level spot on top, at an elevation of 8,800 feet. It's possible to break up this long trip by camping in Little Yosemite Valley. (You'll need a wilderness permit.) 17 miles/10–14 hr. Very strenuous. Happy Isles/shuttle-bus stop 16.

Lower Yosemite Fall   Lower Yosemite Fall is a 320-foot section of Yosemite Fall, but it packs the accumulated punch of the entire 2,425-foot waterfall, and from early spring to midsummer you're likely to get wet. You can also take this trip from Yosemite Village by following the path from the Valley Visitor Center to the Lower Yosemite Fall trail head. Add another half-mile or 40 minutes each way. This walk is wheelchair accessible with assistance. 0.5 miles/30 min. Easy. From shuttle bus stop 6, follow the paved path from the Yosemite Falls parking area to the base of this waterfall.

Mirror Lake   This paved trail climbs 60 feet along the west side of Tenaya Creek to the aptly named Mirror Lake, where overhanging rock formations reflect in the lake's still surface. This trail connects with a delightful 3-mile loop around the lake, which is wheelchair accessible. 2 miles/1 hr. Easy. Shuttle-bus stop 17.

Mist Trail to Vernal Fall 😊😊😊   This hike begins on the famous 211-mile John Muir Trail, a trail that eventually ends on Mount Whitney in Sequoia & Kings Canyon National Parks. From the Happy Isles Bridge, the trail climbs 400 feet to the Vernal Fall Bridge, which offers water and restrooms, as well as a good view of what lies ahead. From this point, you can either take a series of switchbacks along the side of the mountain, or you can ascend the Mist Trail (our preference), which is a steep climb with 500 steps— it's wet, picturesque, and refreshing. The Mist Trail is so named because the spray from the fall drenches anyone who tackles this route, especially in spring. Be warned—it's slick and requires careful

Hiking Trails Near Yosemite Valley

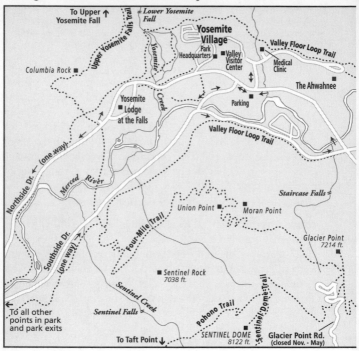

placement of your feet. Once you reach the top, you can relax on a series of smooth granite beaches and soak in the cool, refreshing water before hiking back down.

3 miles/2–3 hr. Moderate to strenuous. From Happy Isles/shuttle-bus stop. 16, walk to the Happy Isles Bridge. Cross the bridge and follow the signs to the trail.

Panorama Trail   From Glacier Point, this trail drops 3,200 feet. At one of its prettiest points, about 1.5 miles from Glacier Point, it crosses Illilouette Fall. The path continues along the Panorama Cliff and eventually winds up at Nevada Fall, where it's a straight descent to Yosemite Valley via the Mist or John Muir trails. You can hike this trail in conjunction with the Four-Mile Trail, and it's also possible to take a bus to Glacier Point and hike only one-way.

9 miles one-way/4–6 hr. one-way. Moderate to strenuous. The hike begins at Glacier Point, at the east end of the parking area.

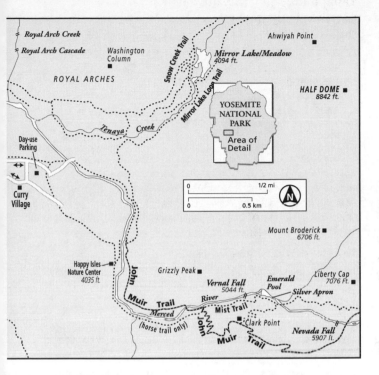

Upper Yosemite Fall Climb this 2,700-foot trail and you'll be rewarded with spectacular views from the ledge above the fall. Take it slow, rest often, and absorb the scenery as you ascend higher and higher above the valley. One mile (and 1,000 feet!) up, you'll reach Columbia Rock, which offers a good view. The rest of the trail dips and climbs, and you'll get a bit of mist from the fall above. The last quarter mile is very rocky and steep, with a series of tortuous, seemingly endless switchbacks that ascend through underbrush before opening at a clearing near the top of the fall. But beware—the view here can induce vertigo. After completing the trail, it's a worthwhile walk upstream to see the creek before it takes its half-mile tumble to the valley floor below. Hikers with the proper permits and equipment can stay here overnight. See chapter 5, "Where to Stay & Eat in Yosemite."

7.2 miles/6–8 hr. Strenuous. Shuttle bus to stop 7; the trail head is next to Camp 4 Walk-in Campground, behind Yosemite Lodge.

SOUTH OF THE VALLEY

Chilnualna Falls from Wawona   One of the tallest falls outside Yosemite Valley, the fall cascades down two chutes. The cascade at the bottom is narrower and packs a real punch after a wet winter. A series of switchbacks leads to the top fall. You may be splashed a bit once you reach the falls, but the trail itself is pretty dry.

8 miles/6 hr. Moderate. From Wawona, take Chilnualna Rd., just north of the Merced River's south fork, until it dead-ends at "The Redwoods," about 1.3 miles. This is the trail head.

Grizzly Giant   This is the walking alternative to the Mariposa Grove tram tour described in chapter 3. It's a nice stroll to see an impressive tree, and the hike climbs only 400 feet. Unfortunately, this walk isn't officially wheelchair accessible.

1.6 miles/1½ hr. Easy. The trail begins at a sign near the map dispenser at the east end of the Mariposa Grove parking lot.

Mariposa Grove   This hike sounds long, but there's a one-way option in the summer that uses the Wawona shuttle bus for the return trip. The trail climbs through a forest and then ascends the Wawona Dome and Wawona Basin, both of which provide excellent views.

13+ miles/1 long day; with shuttle, about half that. Moderate to strenuous. Park at the Wawona Store parking area and walk east 0.25 miles to Forest Dr. The trail head is on the right.

Sentinel Dome 🌟🌟   At the starting point, you'll be able to see Sentinel Dome on your left. The trail descends slightly; at the first fork, bear right. The way winds through manzanita and pine trees before beginning its ascent. It's a steep scramble to the top of Sentinel Dome, and you have to leave the trail on the north (left) side to clamber up. The view from the top offers a 180-degree panorama of Yosemite Valley, one of the most stunning views in a park that's full of them.

2.2 miles/2–3 hr. Moderate. Take Glacier Point Rd. to the Sentinel Dome parking lot, about 3 miles from Glacier Point.

Taft Point   The walk to Taft Point is not demanding, and it crosses a broad meadow dotted by wildflowers in early summer. Near Taft Point, note the deep chasms, known as "fissures," in the rock. Some of the cracks are 40 feet long and 20 feet wide at the top and 100 feet deep. The wall of Yosemite actually overhangs the narrow ravine below, and if you carefully peer over the cliff, you'll notice that your head is on the opposite side of a stream running far beneath you. A small pipe railing farther on marks the 6-by-3-foot Taft Point overlook hanging over Yosemite Valley.

2.2 miles/2 hr. Moderate. The trail head begins at the same point as the hike to Sentinel Dome (see above). At the fork, head left.

Wawona Meadow Loop   This relaxing stroll encircles Wawona Meadow, curving around at its east end and heading back toward the road. It then crosses the highway and winds through forest until it returns to the Wawona Hotel. Some cars still use this road, so keep your eyes and ears open. This trail is also open to pets.

3.5 miles/1½ hr. Easy. Take the dirt road through the Wawona golf course and walk about 50 yards to the trail.

NORTH OF THE VALLEY

Some of the day hikes discussed below can also be done as overnight backpacking trips; see "Exploring the Backcountry," later in this chapter.

Cathedral Lakes   These lakes are set in granite bowls cut by glaciers. The peaks and domes around both Lower and Upper Cathedral Lakes are well worth the hike. Lower Cathedral Lake is next to Cathedral Peak and is a good place to stop for a snack before heading up the hill to enjoy the upper lake.

8 miles/4–6 hr. Moderate. The trail head is off Tioga Rd., at the west end of Tuolumne Meadows, west of Budd Creek.

Cloud's Rest   This hike descends through a wooded area, heading toward Sunrise Lakes. Ascend out of Tenaya Canyon and bear right at the junction (watch for the signposts); the vistas will appear almost at once. The sight line to your destination will be clear—a good thing, since the trail is sketchy at this point. The last stretch to the top is a little spooky, with sheer drops on each side, but your perseverance will be amply rewarded with spectacular views of the park's granite domes. Overnight stays (backcountry permit required) offer the added incentive of beautiful sunrises.

14 miles/7 hr. Strenuous. Take CA 120 to Tenaya Lake. The trail begins at the parking area on the east side of the road near the southwest end of the lake.

Dog Lake 🐾🐾   This easy climb through forests offers great views of Mount Dana. Dog Lake is warm, shallow, and great for swimming.

3 miles/1 hr. Easy. Take CA 120 to the access road for Tuolumne Lodge. Pass the ranger station and park at a parking lot on the left. Walk north (back toward the hwy.) up an embankment and cross CA 120 to find Dog Lake Trail.

Backcountry Hikes in Yosemite

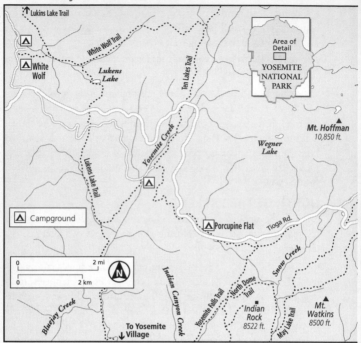

Elizabeth Lake ✸✸✸ This popular day hike attracts a slew of people, which can be a bummer, but it's magnificent and beautiful nonetheless—Elizabeth Lake glistens like ice. Don't forget your camera and some extra film—the route is one long Kodak moment.

6 miles/3 hr. Moderate. Take CA 120 to the group camping area of Tuolumne Meadows Campground, where the trail begins.

Gaylor Lakes This trail begins with a climb, then descends to an alpine lake. It's a particularly pretty hike in summer, when the mountainsides are dotted with wildflowers.

6 miles/3 hr. Moderate. Take CA 120 to Tioga Pass. The trail head is on the northwest side of the road.

Glen Aulin This hike takes you to an impressive waterfall with grand views along the way. Start by heading across a flat meadow toward Soda Springs and Glen Aulin. The trail is well marked, and signs along the way do a good job of describing the area's history.

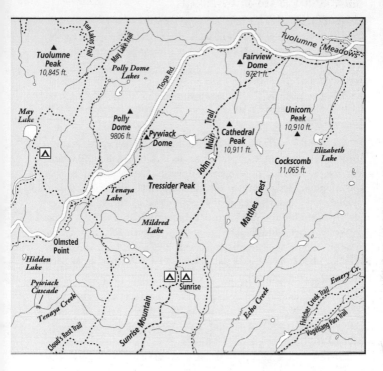

This was once the old Tioga Road, which was built in 1883 to serve the Great Sierra Mine in Tioga Pass. This walk offers a view of the landmarks of Tuolumne Meadows. Behind you, Lembert Dome rises almost 900 feet above the meadow. About 0.4 miles from the trail head, the road forks; head right up the grassy slope. In less than 500 feet is a trail that leaves the road on the right and a steel sign that says GLEN AULIN IS 4.7 MILES AHEAD. This is the trail to take. Along the way you'll pass Fairview Dome, Cathedral Peak, and Unicorn Peak. The crashing noise you'll hear in early to midsummer is Tuolumne Falls, a cascade of water that drops 12 feet, then 40 feet down a series of ledges. From here you can see a nearby High Sierra camp. There's also a hikers' camp if you want to spend the night.

10.4 miles/1 long day. Strenuous. Take CA 120 toward Tuolumne Meadows, about 1 mile east of the Tuolumne Meadows Visitor Center and just a few yards east of the bridge over the Tuolumne River. Follow a marked turnoff and take the paved road on your left. The trail head begins about 0.3 miles ahead, at a road that turns right and heads up a hill toward the stables.

Lembert Dome   This hike offers a bird's-eye view of Tuolumne Meadows—a great vista. A well-marked trail leads you to the top of the dome, and from there you'll see the peaks that encircle the valley, plus get good views of this lovely meadow. It's a great place to watch sunrises and sunsets.

2.8 miles/2 hr. Moderate. The trail head is at a parking lot north of CA 120 in Tuolumne Meadows at rd. marker T-32. Follow the nature trail that starts here and take off at marker no. 2.

May Lake 🐾🐾   Winding through forests and granite, this picturesque hike offers ample opportunities to fish, but swimming is not allowed. Located in the center of Yosemite National Park, it is a good jumping-off point for other high-country hikes. There are numerous peaks surrounding the lake, including the 10,855-foot-high Mount Hoffman, which rises behind the lake. There is a High Sierra camp here, and a hikers' camp on the south side of the lake.

2.5 miles/1 hr. Easy. Take CA 120 east past White Wolf; turn off at rd. marker T-21 and drive 2 miles to the May Lake parking area.

Mono Pass   You'll pass some historical cabin sites, then hike down to Walker Lake, and return via the same route. The hike loops into the Inyo National Forest and the Ansel Adams Wilderness and climbs to an elevation of 10,600 feet. There's a stupendous view of Mono Lake from the top of the trail.

8.5 miles/4–6 hr. Moderate to strenuous. The trail head for this hike is on the south side of CA 120 as you enter the park from Lee Vining. Drive about 1.5 miles from the park entrance to Dana Meadows, where the trail begins on an abandoned road and up alongside Parker Creek Pass.

Mount Dana   This climb is an in-your-face reminder that Mount Dana is Yosemite's second-highest peak. The mountain rises 13,053 feet and the trail gains a whopping 3,100 feet in 3 miles. The views at the top are wonderful, and once you catch your breath you can stand upright again and stare at them in awe. You can see Mono Lake from the summit. In summer, wildflowers add to this hike's beauty.

5.8 miles/5 hr. Very strenuous. The trail head is on the southeast side of CA 120 at Tioga Pass.

North Dome   Walk south down the abandoned road toward the Porcupine Creek Campground. A mile past the campground the trail hits a junction with the Tenaya Creek and Tuolumne Meadows Trail. Pass a junction toward Yosemite Falls and head uphill toward North Dome. The ascent is treacherous because of loose gravel, but from the top you can catch an all-encompassing view of Yosemite Valley, second only to the view from Half Dome.

10 miles/5 hr. Moderate. Take CA 120 east to the Porcupine Flat Campground, past White Wolf. About 1 mile past the campground is a sign for Porcupine Creek at a closed rd. Park in the designated area.

Polly Dome Lake *(Finds)*   This hike is easily the road least traveled. The trip to Polly Dome Lake is a breeze and you'll find nary another traveler in sight. There are several lakes beneath Polly Dome that can accommodate camping. The trail fades in and out, so watch for markers. It crosses a rocky area en route, then skirts southeast at a pond located just after the rocky section. Polly Dome Lake is at the base of—you guessed it—Polly Dome, a visual aid to help hikers stay the course.

12.5 miles/6 hr. Easy to moderate. Take CA 120 past White Wolf to Tenaya Lake. Drive about 0.5 miles to a picnic area midway along the lake. The trail head is across the rd. from the picnic area.

Soda Springs   This trail crosses Tuolumne Meadows, and then crosses Tuolumne River on a wooden bridge. It's peaceful and beautiful, with the sound of the river gurgling along as it winds slowly through the wide expanse of Tuolumne Meadows. The trail leads to a carbonated spring where you can taste the water, although it gets mixed reviews. Parsons Lodge, an activity center, is close by. Also nearby is the historic McCauley Cabin, which is used for employee housing in the summer.

1.5 miles/1 hr. Easy. 2 trail heads: 1 is at a crosswalk just east of the Tuolumne Meadows Visitor Center. The other leaves from a parking lot north of CA 120 at rd. marker T-32. Follow the gravel rd. around a locked gate.

Sunrise Lakes   This hike leads through quiet wooded glades while affording occasional glimpses of distant vistas. Look for a sign that says SUNRISE; then follow the level road to Tenaya Creek, cross the creek, and follow the trail to the right. The hike parallels Tenaya Creek for about a quarter mile, then moves away through a wooded area and climbs gently up a rocky rise. After a while, the trail descends quickly to the outlet of Mildred Lake. There you'll be able to see Mount Hoffmann, Tuolumne Peak, and Tenaya Canyon. At the halfway mark, the trail passes through a hemlock grove, and comes to a junction. Head left. (The trail on the right goes toward Cloud's Rest.) About a quarter mile from the junction you'll reach Lower Sunrise Lake, tucked into the slope of Sunrise Mountain. The trail climbs past Middle Sunrise Lake and continues upward along a cascading creek coming from Upper Sunrise Lake. The trail follows the lake's shore and opens in less than a half-mile onto a wide, bare, sandy pass. Before you is the snowcapped Clark Range. The trail begins its descent, sharply switching back and forth in some places. There is a High Sierra camp and backpackers' camp a short distance above Upper Sunrise Lake.

7–8 miles/5–8 hr. Moderate to strenuous. Take CA 120 to Tenaya Lake. The trail begins in the parking area on the east side of the rd. near the southwest end of the lake.

Tioga Lake to Dana Lake   This is a less-crowded alternative to the above hike to Mount Dana. This particular trail doesn't reach the summit of the mountain, although experienced hikers can reach it on the Mount Dana Trail (see above). The trail is not maintained, although it is fairly visible. This area is easily damaged, so be sure to tread lightly. Mount Dana looms large from the lake's shore.

4.6 miles/2 hr. Moderate to strenuous. Take CA 120 to Tioga Lake. The trail head is on the west side of the lake, about a mile east of the pass.

2 Exploring the Backcountry

Of the more than 3 million people who visit Yosemite each year, 95% never leave the valley, but the brave 5% who do so are well rewarded. A wild, lonelier Yosemite awaits just a few miles from the crowds, where you'll find some of the most grandiose landscape in the Sierra. Most hikers, especially serious backpackers, head into the high country—a backpacking paradise. Tioga Pass via CA 120 is the gateway to the high country. Once through the pass, the high country presents meadows of wildflowers, stark granite domes, and shimmering rivers and lakes.

Most backpackers set out on their own, as we discuss below, but guided backpacking trips (including overnight trips) are also available with the respected **Yosemite Mountaineering School** (✆ **209/ 372-8344;** www.yosemitemountaineering.com). Techniques and skills are taught along the way, and the student-to-instructor ratio usually does not exceed 7 to 1. Meals are included on longer trips. Private trips are available, as is transportation to and from the trail heads. Gear is available for rent.

A car is much more vital in Yosemite's high country than it is in the valley. There is a once-a-day shuttle from the valley to Tuolumne Meadows. The bus leaves the valley at 8am and will let you off anywhere along the route. The driver waits in Tuolumne Meadows for 2 hours before heading back to the valley, where the bus arrives at about 4pm. The fare is about $15 one-way, slightly less for those who hop off midway. In addition, the park offers a summer-only shuttle bus from Olmstead Point to Tioga Pass, with stops at Tuolumne Lodge, Tuolumne Campground, and Tuolumne Visitor Center.

Tuolumne Meadows is a wide, grassy expanse bordered by the Tuolumne River and tall mountains. Several peaks rise high overhead and offer challenging hiking and rock climbing. In spring and midsummer, the meadow fills with wildflowers and turns an emerald green. Fishing in the river is popular, and a number of hikes begin in the meadows. There is a general store that stocks last-minute hiking supplies, a slew of canvas tent-cabins (often all full in summer), and a restaurant.

In addition to Tuolumne Meadows, **Tenaya Lake,** set in a bowl of granite surrounded by sheer slopes, is a beautiful destination spot en route to the high country. Tenaya Lake offers canoeing, hiking, fishing, and sailing. It's also open to swimming for those who don't mind dunking in the chilly water—it generally remains frigid until late summer. There's ample parking and a picnic area, and many hikes lead from here to the high country. **White Wolf** is midway between the valley and Tuolumne Meadows (west of Tenaya Lake). It encompasses a campground, canvas tent-cabins, a small store, and a restaurant. The scenery here is less dramatic, but it serves as a starting point for many hikers going into the Hetch Hetchy area. This region is accessible only by snowshoeing or cross-country skiing in the winter.

Like any backcountry experience, staying in the high country—or anyplace outside the valley—requires advance planning and, if you're a beginner, a reasonable itinerary. Planning a 5-day excursion your first time out wouldn't be wise. But an overnighter, or 2 nights out, is reasonable, and Yosemite has hikes that can accommodate and reward those who venture—even briefly—off the well-paved path.

In addition, the park has five **High Sierra camps** that provide food and shelter, allowing hikers to shun heavy backpacking gear with the knowledge that someone a few miles ahead has everything under control. All camps fill quickly and advance reservations are necessary. The camps—May Lake, Glen Aulin, Vogelsang, Sunrise Lakes, Merced Lake, and Tuolumne—are situated about a day's walk apart, and each is a sort of rustic resort. Tent-cabins are furnished with steel bunk beds, wood stoves, and a folding table and chairs. Beds include a mattress, three blankets, a comforter, and a pillow. Soap and candles are also provided. Most tents sleep four, but some accommodate only two people. This means you'll often be sharing your tent with strangers, but the camps tend to attract people who rank high on the camaraderie scale, so that's not usually a problem. Breakfast and dinner are served family style in a dining tent. The food is yummy and portions are generous. One dinner meal included pasta, filet mignon, soup and salad, eggplant Parmesan, and cookies. Breakfast is substantial as well. Box lunches are available for an additional charge. All you need to bring is day-hike stuff, plus a flashlight, personal toiletries, something to sleep in, a change of underclothes, and bed linen.

Each camp accommodates 30 to 60 guests; demand exceeds supply, so accommodations are assigned by a lottery. Requests are accepted in fall and assigned in winter to the lucky few. Cancellations are frequent, however, so it's worth a last-minute call to see if space is available at any of the camps. The camps offer a meals-only option (reservations required) if you want to bring your own tent and eat at the camp. For information or to request an application for High Sierra camp accommodations, call ℭ **559/253-5676** or visit **www.yosemitepark.com**. Applications are accepted from November 1 to November 30. The lottery drawing is held in mid-December, and guests are notified by the end of February. Camps are open from mid-June to around Labor Day, conditions permitting. Overnights at the camps cost $126 per person for meals (breakfast and dinner) and lodging.

PREPARING FOR YOUR BACKCOUNTRY TRIP

The most important thing to do is get a detailed topographical map before setting out on any overnight hike. These are available at many Yosemite stores, visitor centers, ranger stations, and the Wilderness Center in Yosemite Valley.

PERMITS & FEES   All overnight backpacking stays require a wilderness permit, available by phone, by mail, or in the park. Permits can be reserved 2 days to 4 months in advance and cost $5 for each individual on the permit. Reservations are accepted, usually beginning in late winter. Call ℭ **209/372-0740** or write to Wilderness Permits, P.O. Box 545, Yosemite National Park, CA 95389.

If advance planning isn't your style, first-come/first-served permits are available up to 24 hours before your trip. Permit stations are located at the Yosemite Valley Wilderness Center, Wawona Information Station, Big Oak Flat Information Station, Hetch Hetchy Entrance Station, and Tuolumne Meadows Information Station. (Many of these are open summer-only; Badger Pass is the lone winter-only permit station.) Permits for the popular trails, such as those leading to Half Dome, Little Yosemite Valley, and Cloud's Rest, go quickly. Call ℭ **209/372-0200** for permit station locations and hours.

To get a permit, you must provide a name, address, telephone number, the number of people in your party, the method of travel (snowshoe, horse, foot), the number of horses or other pack animals if applicable, start and end dates, start and end trail heads, and principal destination. Include alternative dates and trail heads as well. Do not neglect getting a permit. You may hike for a week and never run into a ranger, but one is guaranteed to show up and ask to see your permit just as you are re-entering civilization.

SPECIAL REGULATIONS & ETIQUETTE   Campfires are not allowed above 9,600 feet, and everything you take in must be packed out. Backpackers must take bear-proof canisters for storing food. They can be rented for $5 a trip at the Yosemite Valley Wilderness Center and at several other park locations.

OVERNIGHT HIKES

All hikers should purchase a good topographical map before embarking on any overnight hike. They are available at stores, visitor centers, and ranger stations throughout Yosemite National Park. Bears live in the high country, so stay alert. In the summer months, mosquitoes are public enemy number one, so bring plenty of repellent. Also pack sunscreen, since much of Yosemite's high country is on granite, above the tree line. Stay off high peaks during thunderstorms, and don't attempt a climb if it looks as though a storm is rolling in. The peaks are magnets for lightning. And finally, trail heads along Tioga Road are accessible only by snowshoes or cross-country skis in winter, as the road is usually closed because of snow from November until June.

Chilnualna Lakes/Buena Vista Peak Loop   Although rather difficult, this trek is satisfying, as it takes you from a stunning waterfall through meadows and forests to some lovely lakes. The first day's hike is 8 miles, to Chilnualna Falls, one of the park's tallest falls outside the valley. It's a strenuous climb up. The bottom fall tumbles down a narrow chute, and 50 feet up is yet another fall; the combination can be quite a vision in spring with a strong winter runoff. Above the falls, the trail ascends via switchbacks up a gorge to a junction. One route will lead through forests toward Bridalveil Campground, the other toward Chilnualna Lakes. Take the Chilnualna Lakes route. Just below this junction are several nice places to camp overnight. There are also a number of nearby swimming holes. From here, it's a climb along the headwaters of the creek to a set of high-altitude lakes. About 2.5 miles up is Grouse Lake Creek. This can be a tough cross during high water, and the rock is very

Backpacking for Beginners

Backpacking requires more preparation than many other sports, including minute attention to detail. Everything you need for food, clothing, and shelter must be carried with you; the longer the trip, the more planning is needed. It's important to be thorough, and it's also important to be conscientious when it comes to weight. First and foremost, the most important gear is what's on your back and on your feet—good boots and a sturdy pack are a necessity. You'll also need a good sleeping bag and sleeping pad. Packs generally come in two types: internal and external frames. Opinions vary over which is best; external-frame packs are slightly cheaper, and internal frame packs are better for long distances or trails that twist and turn. Internal-frame packs distribute weight more evenly and cinch tight across your hips, making them more comfortable for long hauls. Try on as many packs as possible. Look for wide shoulder straps, lumbar support, and a wide hip belt. Make sure it feels good and ask lots of questions. If your questions are not answered with painstaking detail so that you feel sure and secure, move on. An uncomfortable or poorly fitting pack is a potential nightmare on a backcountry trip.

Now for the fun stuff—packing everything you'll need to subsist inside this bag you've bought. One easy method: Pull out everything you could possibly want, and then return most of it from whence it came. You really don't need three pairs of pants or 10 T-shirts.

As for food, a mix of dried foods (pastas, lentils, beans, dried meats, and fruit), crackers, cereal, trail mix (nuts, raisins, and M&Ms), granola bars, envelopes of pre-made soups, and plastic jars of peanut butter and jelly work great. One guy I know hiked the Appalachian Trail with entire loaves of peanut butter and jelly sandwiches, all pre-made and repacked into the bread bag. It worked. And don't forget about water. There is plenty of water in Yosemite's high country, but you'll need to treat it to prevent *Giardia*. Don't take chances: This little bug is one painful parasite to ingest.

slick, so be careful. Head north (left) for about a half-mile after the crossing toward Turner Meadows. At the next junction, head right (east) toward Chilnualna Lakes, about 5 miles away. Buena Vista Peak rises above the lakes. Campsites are plentiful in this area. From the lakes, head up into 9,040-foot Buena Vista Pass. At the pass, head south on Buena Vista Trail toward Royal Arch Lake. The next junction goes right (west) toward Johnson, Crescent, and Grouse lakes. After Grouse Lake is the Grouse Lake Creek crossing and the return trail to Chilnualna Falls and the parking area.

28 miles/4 days. Moderate to strenuous. Take CA 41 to Wawona in Yosemite National Park. Turn east on Chilnualna Rd. and stay on this road for about 1.3 miles until you reach "The Redwoods," where the road ends. This is the trail head.

Ten Lakes Trail The trail is well marked and picturesque, with lots of rocks to climb around on and several lakes for swimming. The trail offers some great fishing for brook and rainbow trout. Mosquitoes can be a major deterrent here in summer. Backpackers camp at the designated campground at May Lake or in an undeveloped spot at least a quarter-mile from the shore. There are numerous places to camp, so it's best to discuss options with a ranger.

12.8 miles/2 days. Moderate. On CA 120 east, pass the White Wolf Campground to the trail head parking lot, just before a bridge and Yosemite Creek sign. The trail head is on the north side of the rd.

Tuolumne Meadows to Agnew Meadows Along the John Muir Trail This high-altitude climb offers visitors a weekend getaway that leaves flatlanders breathless and displays some of the eastern Sierra's most pristine beauty. Be warned—it's a real heart-thumper. You'll trek through Donohue Pass at 11,056 feet. From the pass it's mostly downhill. Campers should discuss the numerous overnight options with a park ranger before heading out.

28 miles/3 days. Strenuous. The trail head begins where the above hike (Ten Lakes Trail) ends, or take CA 120 to Tuolumne Meadows and the signed trail head parking area for the John Muir/Pacific Crest Trail/Lyell Fork hikes.

Yosemite Creek This hike approaches Yosemite Falls from behind and ends up at the same place as the Upper Yosemite Fall hike described in earlier in this chapter, without the steep climb up from the valley floor. After hiking 2 miles, you'll see the Yosemite Creek Campground. Hike through the campground to the Yosemite Falls Trail. In about three-quarters of a mile, you'll hit another junction. Head left (south) and hike for another 4 miles to Upper Yosemite Fall. The view from here is heart-stopping. The valley looks like something out of Disneyland with its tiny lodges, people, and cars far below. The

Impressions

Thousands of tired, nerve-shaken, overcivilized people are beginning to find out that going to the mountains is going home; that wilderness is a necessity.

—John Muir

waterfall is surrounded by slick rock, so be careful, especially in wet conditions; it seems that every year someone slips over the edge into the abyss below. You can hike back the way you came, or head down the path to the valley if you've got a shuttle system set up or someone to take you back to your car. As with all overnight hikes, discuss camping options with a ranger before heading out.

17 miles/1–2 days. Moderate to strenuous. Take CA 120 east past the White Wolf Campground to the trail head, which is just before a bridge sign for Yosemite Creek. The trail head is on the south side of the highway.

Yosemite Valley to Tuolumne Meadows along the John Muir Trail   The trail is well marked and heads from the valley floor past Half Dome and then up to Cathedral Peak. Cathedral Lakes are nearby and worth a side trip. Camp at Tuolumne Meadows.

22 miles/2 days. Moderate to strenuous. The trail begins in the valley at the Happy Isles parking area.

SIDE TRIPS FROM HIGH SIERRA CAMPS

Glen Aulin High Sierra Camp to Waterwheel Falls   This walk is long and arduous but takes you to six major waterfalls along the Tuolumne. You'll climb about 1,000 feet along open ledges on the river. There's a lot to see, so get an early start. The trail switches along the noisy river, plunges into a forest, and meanders across a meadow. The most notable waterfalls begin about 1.5 miles into the hike and range from long ribbons to 50-foot-long, 20-foot-wide masses of white water. The trail descends through a canyon. Watch for signs to Glen Aulin (about 3.5 miles away). You'll see LeConte Falls on your left beyond a few campsites. It cascades in broad, thin sheets of water, some stretching 30 feet wide as they flow down steeply sloping ledges along the river. A half-mile past LeConte is the top of Waterwheel Falls, a set of long, narrow falls that roar through a trough in the ledge to the left of the trail. With enough water and force, some of the water hits the ledge rock with sufficient force to propel it upward and back in a circle, like a pinwheel. Backward waterwheels are rare and should not be confused with the upward and forward spinning waterwheel of LeConte Falls. You can climb down to and back from Waterwheel Falls—it'll add a steep half-mile to your trip—before returning to Glen Aulin.

7.6 miles/8 hr. Strenuous (but worth it). Cross Conness Creek and the trail head is on your left about 30 ft. ahead.

Sunrise High Sierra Camp to Upper Cathedral Lake   Views of the stunning Cathedral Peak highlight this hike. Descend the stone steps to the John Muir Trail along the north side of a meadow. The trail skirts the meadow and crosses several small creeks. Stick to the John Muir Trail, which will bring you to a branch of Cathedral Fork, which has a riverbed lined with rust-colored rocks. After 2 miles, the trail falls away from the creek and toward Columbia Finger, climbing a rocky slope that quickly levels off. You'll see a variety of peaks along the way, and toward the end, when Cathedral Peak comes into view, you'll be surrounded by 2-mile-high pinnacles that somehow escaped the prehistoric glaciers. The trail descends through a meadow, then on to Upper Cathedral Lake. The trek back to camp offers stunning views from the reverse perspective.

10 miles/6–8 hr. Moderate to strenuous. The hike begins next to the dining tent.

Vogelsang High Sierra Camp to Vogelsang Pass   This hike offers broad views of an assortment of peaks. Turn left from the trail where it crosses the creek (just past the intersection of the pass trail and the camp trail), walk 50 feet upstream, and cross the creek. You'll find nothing but spectacular views. The two towers of Vogelsang Peak lie ahead, stretched apart like some enormous saddle. This walk offers views of Vogelsang Lake. The rough slopes of Vogelsang Peak and Vogelsang Pass are straight ahead. (Vogelsang Peak is the one on the right.) A 50-foot-wide pond surrounded by pinkish granite marks the top of the pass. Cross to the north side for one of the most spectacular views in the High Sierra. Walk a few feet more, to the point where the trail begins to descend toward Lewis Creek, and a magnificent panorama will greet you: 12,080-foot Parson's Peak; 12,503-foot Simmons Peak; 12,960-foot Mount Maclure; the wide 12,561-foot Mount Florence; the summits of Clark Range, Triple Divide, and Merced peaks; the aptly named Red and Gray peaks; and Mount Clark. Look down and you'll see the blue-green Bernice Lake.

3 miles/2–3 hr. Moderate to strenuous. The walk begins on the west side of the dining tent and descends to Fletcher Creek.

3 Other Sports & Activities

About the only thing you can't do in Yosemite is surf. In addition to sightseeing, Yosemite is a great place to bike, ski, rock climb, fish, and even golf.

BICYCLING   There are 12 miles of designated bike trails in the eastern end of Yosemite Valley, which is the best place to ride since roads and shuttle-bus routes are usually crowded and dangerous for bicyclists. Children under 18 are required by law to wear helmets. During the summer, single-speed bikes can be rented by the hour ($7.50) or the day ($24.50) at Curry Village (© 209/372-8319). Year-round, you can rent bikes at Yosemite Lodge (© 209/372-1208). Bike rentals include helmets for all ages.

CROSS-COUNTRY SKIING   The park has more than 350 miles of skiable trails and roads, including 25 miles of machine-groomed track and 90 miles of marked trails in the Badger Pass area. Equipment rentals, lessons (including excellent beginner lessons), and day and overnight ski tours are available from **Badger Pass Cross-Country Center and Ski School** (© 209/372-8444; www.yosemitepark.com, click the link for "activities").

FISHING   Several species of trout are found in Yosemite's streams. Guided fly-fishing trips in Yosemite for all levels are available from **Yosemite Guides** (© 877/425-3366; www.yosemiteguides.com). California fishing licenses are required for everyone 16 and older; information is available from the **California State Department of Fish and Game** (© 559/222-3761; www.dfg.ca.gov). There are also special fishing regulations in Yosemite Valley; get information at the visitor centers.

GOLF   There's one golf course in the park and several others nearby. **Wawona** (© 209/375-6572) sports a 9-hole, par-35 course that alternates between meadows and fairways. Just outside the park, the 18-hole **Sierra Meadows Ranch Course** (© 559/683-3388) is in Oakhurst. Call for current greens fees and other information.

HORSEBACK RIDING   Several companies offer guided horseback rides in and just outside the national park, with rates starting at about $25 for 1 hour, $40 for 2 hours, and $75 for a half-day. **Yosemite Stables** (© 209/372-8348) offers rides from Yosemite Valley, Tuolumne Meadows, and Wawona, and leads multiday pack trips into the backcountry (call for details). **Yosemite Trails Pack Station** (© 559/683-7611) offers riding just south of Wawona, and

Minarets Pack Station (© 559/868-3405; www.highsierrapackers. org/min.htm) leads day trips to Yosemite and the Ansel Adams Wilderness.

ICE SKATING   The outdoor ice rink at Curry Village, with great views of Half Dome and Glacier Point, is open from early November to March, weather permitting. Admission costs $6.50 for adults and $5 for children, with skate rental $3.25. Check with park visitor centers for the current hours (© 209/372-0200).

RAFTING   A raft-rental shop is located at Curry Village (© 209/ 372-8319). Daily fees are $13.50 for adults, $11.50 for children under 13. Fees include a raft, paddles, mandatory life preservers, and transportation from Sentinel Beach to Curry Village. Swift currents and cold water can be deadly. Talk with rangers and shop people before venturing out to be sure you're planning a trip that's within your capabilities.

ROCK CLIMBING   Yosemite is considered one of the world's premier playgrounds for experienced rock climbers and wannabes. The **Yosemite Mountaineering School** (© 209/372-8344; www. yosemitemountaineering.com) provides instruction for beginning, intermediate, and advanced climbers in the valley and Tuolumne Meadows, April through October. Classes last from a day to a week, and private lessons are available. All equipment is provided, and rates vary according to the class or program.

SKIING   Yosemite's **Badger Pass Ski Area** (© 209/372-8430; www.yosemitepark.com) is usually open from Thanksgiving to Easter Sunday, weather permitting. This small resort, located 22 miles from Yosemite Valley, was established in 1935. There are 10 runs, rated 35% beginner, 50% intermediate, and 15% advanced; with a vertical drop of 800 feet from the highest point of 8,000 feet. There are five lifts—one triple chair, three double chairs, and a cable tow. Full-day adult lift tickets cost $35, and full-day lift tickets for kids 12 and under are $18; half-day tickets are $25 and $15, respectively.

Kids ESPECIALLY FOR KIDS

Many of the activities listed in this section have special programs for children, including rock climbing and ski lessons. In addition, Yosemite offers Little Cub and Junior Ranger programs, and special walks and activities for kids. See "Tips for Travelers with Children," in chapter 2.

The ski area has several casual restaurants, a ski shop, ski repairs, a day lodge, lockers, and an excellent ski school, thanks to "Ski Ambassador" Nic Fiore, a Yosemite ski legend who arrived in the park in 1947 to ski for a season and never left. Fiore became director of the ski school in 1956, and park officials credit Fiore with making Badger Pass what it is today—a family-oriented ski area where generations have learned the art of skiing.

5

Where to Stay & Eat in Yosemite

There is no lack of choices for accommodations in and near Yosemite National Park. Yosemite Valley is the hub for lodging, dining, and other services within the park, and is usually quite crowded in summer, but it offers the best location—close to Yosemite's main attractions and with easy access to the park's shuttle-bus system.

A more narrow scope of choices is available outside the valley, but still within the park: You can camp at Wawona, Tuolumne Meadows, White Wolf, and a host of other campsites; and there are privately owned cabins and bed-and-breakfasts. In addition, there are some delightful (and generally less expensive) accommodations, campgrounds, and restaurants outside the park in the gateway communities of El Portal, Mariposa, Oakhurst, and Groveland.

1 Lodging

INSIDE THE PARK

Lodging in the park is under the auspices of **DNC Parks & Resorts at Yosemite.** Rooms can be reserved up to 366 days in advance (© **559/252-4848;** TTY 209/255-8345). You can make reservation requests online at **www.yosemitepark.com**. Reservations are also accepted by mail at Yosemite Reservations, 6771 N. Palm Ave., Fresno, CA 93704.

In addition, more than 130 private homes in the park can be rented through **The Redwoods in Yosemite,** P.O. Box 2085, Wawona Station, Yosemite National Park, CA 95389 (© **209/375-6666;** www.redwoodsinyosemite.com). Offerings range from rustic cabins to luxurious vacation homes, and all are fully furnished and equipped with linens, cookware, and dishes. Rates range from $175 a night for a one-bedroom cabin to $500 a night or more for a five-bedroom spread; there are usually 3-night minimum stays in summer, and 2-night minimums the rest of the year.

The Ahwahnee 🌟🌟🌟   This hotel's accommodations are fit for a king or queen, and it has hosted both. Queen Elizabeth II slept here, as have U.S. President John F. Kennedy, actor Clint Eastwood, poet Alfred Noyes, and NFL quarterback Steve Young. It's tough to top The Ahwahnee, a six-story cement, concrete, and stone structure that offers beautiful views from nearly every window. The hotel has a number of common rooms on the ground floor. There are three fireplaces large enough to stand in, and the rooms are furnished with large overstuffed sofas and chairs, perfect for reading or playing games after a day of hiking. Guest rooms are upstairs, and the majority of the suites are located on the top floor. Suites include a pair of rooms: one for sleeping and another for sitting. The Sunroom Suite is a bright pair of rooms in lime and yellow with comfy lounges and floor-to-ceiling French windows that open out onto the valley. The Library Room's rich decor includes a fireplace and walls of books. Regular rooms offer a choice of two doubles or one king-size bed, with a couch, plush towels, and snuggly comforters.

Yosemite Valley. ✆ **559/252-4848.** 123 units. $379 guest rooms and cottages; 2-room suites from $859; 3-room suites from $1,238. AE, DC, DISC, MC, V. Parking available, or take the shuttle bus to stop 3. **Amenities:** Restaurant (see "Where to Eat," later in this chapter); bar; outdoor pool; tour desk; limited room service; in-room massage services; babysitting for children out of diapers; dry cleaning; laundry service; express checkout; valet parking. *In room:* TV, coffeemaker.

Curry Village   Curry Village is best known as a mass of more than 400 white canvas tents tightly packed together on the valley's south slope. It was founded in 1899 as a cheap lodging option for valley visitors at a mere $2 a day, but guests can kiss those $2 days goodbye. Still, it's an economical place to crash, and gives you something of the feeling of a camping vacation without the hassle of bringing your own tent. One downside is that these tents are basically canvas affairs, and this is bear country, so you'll need to lock up all foodstuffs and anything that bears might think is food (even toothpaste) in bear-proof lockers (provided free), which may be a healthy walk from your tent-cabin. Curry Village also has just over 100 attractive wood cabins with private bathrooms; about 80 wood cabins that, like the tent-cabins, share a large bathhouse; and a number of motel rooms. Canvas tents have wood floors, sleep two to four people, and are equipped with beds, bedding, dressers, and electrical outlets. The wood cabins are much more substantial (and comfortable), and the motel rooms are just what motel rooms should be—functional and adequate.

Yosemite Valley. ✆ **559/252-4848.** 628 units. Reservations suggested. $69 double tent-cabin; $85 double cabin without bathroom; $93–$108 double cabin with bathroom; $100–$113 double motel room. AE, DC, DISC, MC, V. Parking is available, or take the shuttle bus to stop 13A, 13B, 14, or 20. **Amenities:** 3 dining options (see "Where to Eat," later in this chapter); outdoor pool; raft rentals; bicycle rentals; children's programs; tour desk; mountaineering school; sports shop.

Housekeeping Camp *Value*

A fun, funky place to spend the night, this is the closest thing to camping without pitching a tent. The sites are fence-enclosed tent-cabins built on concrete slabs, each with a table, cupboard, electrical outlets, shelves, a mirror, and lights. The sleeping areas have two single-size bunks and a double bed.

Yosemite Valley. *C* **559/252-4848.** 266 units, all with shared restrooms and shower facilities. Reservations required. $67 per site (up to 4 people; $5 per extra person). Shower house. AE, DC, DISC, MC, V. Closed Nov–Mar. Parking is available, or shuttle stop no. 12. **Amenities:** Grocery store; self-serve laundry.

Tuolumne Meadows Lodge

Not a lodge, but another group of canvas tent-cabins. Like White Wolf Lodge (see below), these have tables and wood-burning stoves and sleep up to four. The lodge is smack-dab in the middle of prime hiking territory that's less crowded than the valley below, but there is still a fair amount of foot and vehicle traffic. This is also home base for wilderness trekkers and backcountry campers.

Tioga Rd., Tuolumne Meadows, Yosemite National Park. *C* **559/252-4848.** 69 canvas tent-cabins, all with shared bathroom and shower house. $75 double; additional $9 per adult or $4 per child. AE, DC, DISC, MC, V. Parking available in an adjacent lot. Closed in winter. From Yosemite Valley, take CA 120 east 60 miles (about 1½ hr.) toward Tioga Pass. **Amenities:** Restaurant (see "Where to Eat," later in this chapter); tour desk; small general store; mountaineering store; gas station; post office; stables.

Wawona Hotel *ඍඍ*

This is a classic Victorian-style hotel made up of six stately white buildings set near towering trees in a green clearing. Don't be surprised if a horse and buggy rounds the driveway by the fishpond—it's that kind of place. What makes it so wonderful? Maybe it's the wide porches, the nearby nine-hole golf course, or the vines of hops cascading from one veranda to the next. The entire place was designated a National Historic Landmark in 1987. Clark Cottage is the oldest building, dating back to 1876, and the main hotel was built in 1879. Rooms are comfortable and quaint with a choice of a double and a twin bed, a king bed, or one double bed. (Most of the latter share bathrooms.) All rooms open onto wide porches and overlook green lawns. Clark Cottage is the most intimate. The main hotel has the widest porches and plenty of Adirondack chairs, and at night the downstairs sunroom hosts a pianist. Check out the whistling maintenance man who hits every high note in the "Star Spangled Banner" while the American flag is hoisted each morning (leaving many bystanders speechless as more than a few Wawona employees chime in to create a veritable whistling orchestra).

Wawona Rd., Wawona, Yosemite National Park. (℃ **559/252-4848**. 104 units, 54 with shared bathroom. $95–$170 double. Additional charge for extra adults $10–$16. AE, DC, DISC, MC, V. From Yosemite Valley, take CA 41 south 27 miles toward Fresno. **Amenities:** Dining room (see "Where to Eat," later in this chapter), lounge; large outdoor pool; golf course; horseback riding; outdoor tennis court; grocery store; gas station.

White Wolf Lodge   Imagine a smaller, quieter, cleaner Curry Village with larger tents, each equipped with a wood-burning stove. This small outpost was bypassed when Tioga Road was rebuilt. White Wolf Lodge is not a lodge, but a cluster of canvas tent-cabins, with a few wooden cabins out front. It's halfway between the valley and the high country, and generally isn't overrun with visitors. It's a popular spot for midweek hikers and weekend stopovers. It can get crowded but retains a homey feeling. Maybe it's the fact that there's no electricity after 11pm when the generator shuts off. Wood cabins all have a private bathroom and resemble a regular motel room, with neat little porches and chairs out front. Canvas cabins beat the Curry Village style by a mile. Each sleeps four in any combination of twin and double beds. There's a table, and the helpful staff will show guests how to work the wood-burning stove. Benches outside give guests a place to rest their weary feet and watch the stars. Bathrooms here are clean, and guests control access to the facilities except for a few midday hours when nearby campers can pay for showers.

Tioga Rd., White Wolf, Yosemite National Park. (℃ **559/252-4848**. 24 canvas tent-cabins, 4 cabins. All canvas cabins share bathroom and shower house. $71–$105 double. Additional charge of $10 per adult in cabins, $9 adult in tents, and $4 per child in cabins or tents. AE, DC, DISC, MC, V. Parking available across a 2-lane rd. Closed in winter. From Yosemite Valley, take CA 120 east 33 miles toward Tioga Pass. **Amenities:** Restaurant (see "Where to Eat," later in this chapter); tiny general store.

Yosemite Lodge at the Falls (*Kids*)   The comfortable and clean rooms here are popular because of the lodge's location, with some units offering views of Yosemite Falls. Rooms have a number of bed configurations, and most rooms have balconies or patios. It's not uncommon to see deer and other wildlife scampering through this area. Spring mornings bring a wonderful orchestra of songbirds and stunning views at sunrise.

Yosemite Valley. (℃ **559/252-4848**. 245 units. Reservations suggested. $113–$162 double. Lower rates Nov–Mar. AE, DC, DISC, MC, V. Parking available or take the shuttle bus to stop 8. **Amenities:** 2 restaurants (see "Where to Eat," later in this chapter), lounge; ice cream stand; large outdoor pool; bicycle rentals; children's programs; tour desk; babysitting; general store.

Yosemite West Lodging   For the unforgettable experience of living in Yosemite National Park (if only for a few nights), instead of just visiting, what could be better than renting a private home, cottage, or condominium unit located right in the park? Yosemite West rents a variety of privately owned accommodations, ranging from fairly simple rooms with one queen-size bed and a kitchenette, suitable for one or two people, to luxurious vacation homes with full-size kitchens, two bathrooms, living rooms, and beds for up to eight people. Kitchens and kitchenettes are fully equipped, all bedding is provided, TVs and VCR/DVD players are on hand, and there are outdoor decks. All units also have gas or wood-burning fireplaces. The homes are in a forested section of the park, about 10 miles from Yosemite Valley and 8 miles from Badger Pass.

P.O. Box 36, Yosemite National Park, CA 95389. (✆ **559/642-2211.** www.yosemite westreservations.com. A fluctuating number of privately owned cottages and private homes. Most units $115–$295 double. Lower rates early Sept to mid-Dec and early Jan to early May. Take CA 41 for 12 miles north of Wawona. *In room:* TV/VCR/DVD player, kitchens, fridge, coffeemaker.

OUTSIDE THE PARK

If you choose to stay outside the park, you'll find a plethora of choices, many of which are less expensive than lodging in the park.

ALONG CALIFORNIA 120 (WEST OF THE PARK)

Yosemite Lodgings is a group of a dozen inns, cabin resorts, and historic hotels near the Big Oak Entrance. Its website is www.staynear yosemite.com.

Friends of Yosemite Lodge ✮✮   The yellow clapboard exterior of this 1990 home southeast of downtown Groveland sheaths a delightful B&B with a tasteful "Yosemite luminaries" theme. Downstairs, the John Muir Room has a lodgepole bed frame on its comfortable king, and books about Muir himself, a Yosemite fanatic and pioneering conservationist. Upstairs, the Ansel Adams room is distinguished by its black-and-white photographs by Adams, of course, and the Jenny Curry Room is frillier, with a skylight and a vanity next to the bed. The suite is a converted mother-in-law apartment with its own entrance, a kitchen, and inviting decor. Breakfasts here are hearty affairs, with stuffed French toast and fresh ingredients from the inn's lush garden.

13349 Clements Rd., Groveland, CA 95321. ℂ **866/410-4545** or 209/962-4544. www.friendsofyosemitelodge.com. 4 units, including 1 suite. $169–$189 double; $275 suite. (A one-time donation of $10 to an education-oriented nonprofit is also required.) Rates include full breakfast (except suite). AE, MC, V. *In room amenities:* A/C, cable TV, kitchen, hair dryer, iron.

Groveland Hotel 𝒶𝒶   There's enough history, good food, and conversation here to give travelers pause before heading into Yosemite. Groveland is about as quaint a town as you can get, and Peggy and Grover Mosley have poured their hearts into making their hotel an elegant but comfortable place to stay. The building was vacant for years and on the verge of crumbling when the Mosleys decided to forgo a quiet retirement from very interesting careers (you'll have to ask for yourself) to renovate and reopen the hotel. They've done a great job, and the hotel is now a historic landmark.

Thwe hotel consists of two buildings—one constructed in 1849 to house gold miners and the other built in 1919 for workers constructing the nearby Hetch Hetchy Dam. Standard rooms are spacious, with feather beds, hair dryers, and phones with dataports. Some have TVs. All rooms are filled with antiques, and have thick down comforters, beds you want to jump on, and plush robes. Suites have large spa bathtubs and fireplaces. Many rooms are named after women of the Sierra and local characters, although Lyle's Room is named for the hotel's resident ghost. Return patrons swear it's true. Then there's Charlie's Room, named for a hard-driving, tobacco-spitting stagecoach driver and farmer. When he died, the townspeople learned that he was a she.

18767 CA 120, Groveland, CA 95321. ℂ **800/273-3314** or 209/962-4000. Fax 209/962-6674. www.groveland.com. 17 units, including 3 suites. $135–$175 double; $225–$275 suite. Extra person $25. Rates include buffet breakfast. AE, DC, DISC, MC, V. Pets accepted with approval. **Amenities:** Small dining room (see "Where to Eat," later in this chapter); 18-hole golf course 1 mile away; tennis courts; room service; safe on premises; stables. *In room:* A/C, TV (in some rooms), dataport, hair dryer.

Hotel Charlotte 𝒶   Walking into the Charlotte is like stepping back in time. Built in 1918 by an Italian immigrant of the same name, it's warm, comfortable, and a good choice for those who enjoy the ambience of a small historic hotel. The hotel's rooms—all upstairs—are small, quaint, and nicely maintained. Several rooms adjoin each other and have connecting bathrooms (perfect for families) with shower/claw-foot tub combos. There's an excellent restaurant, Café Charlotte, and the lobby has a TV and a guest computer with Internet access. (There's also a Wi-Fi network on the premises.)

The pancake buffet breakfast is great—with strong coffee, cereals, fruit, juices, and piping-hot flapjacks.

18736 CA 120, Groveland, CA 95321. © 800/961-7799 or 209/962-6455. Fax 209/962-6254. www.hotelcharlotte.com. 10 units. $89–$129 double. Rates include full breakfast. AE, MC, V. **Amenities:** Restaurant. *In room:* A/C.

Sunset Inn ⋒ *Finds*   Located just 2 miles from Yosemite's entrance gates, the Sunset Inn is the perfect antidote to the hubbub you encounter in the valley. Surrounded by old-growth forest, the inn's 2 acres were once a bustling logging camp, then became a tourist camp, and now are a world apart, complete with a frog pond, chicken coop, and hiking trails in every direction. The three cabins here are not new by any means, but have been lovingly restored by Bill Nickell, the carpenter-innkeeper who owns and operates the place with his wife, Lauren. (They've called the property home since the 1970s.) Each cabin has attractive woodwork, quilts, a wood-burning stove, and a full kitchen. The comfy indoors are matched outdoors with picnic tables, barbecue grills, and porch rockers that are ideal to watch the phenomenon from which the inn took its name. The Nickells also manage a four-bedroom log home a few miles west.

33569 Harden Flat Rd., Groveland, CA 95321. © 888/962-4360 or 209/962-4360. www.sunsetinnusa.com. 3 cabins, 1 vacation home. $130–$200 cabin; $225–$275 vacation home. MC, V. **Amenities:** Playground. *In room:* Kitchen.

Yosemite Rose ⋒⋒   Located on 210 acres of working ranchland, this beautiful Victorian B&B is actually a product of the 21st century: Built in 2000, the inn was modeled after the Mountain View, California, home of Henry Rengstorfer, the 19th-century owner of the spot now known as Silicon Valley. From the public rooms (featuring a pool table, murals, and a player piano) to the grounds (with a stocked fishing pond, stables, and an olive orchard) to the rooms (with top-end soft goods and compelling antiques), innkeeper Katherine Davalle has left little to chance here. A good many of the furnishings here have amazing stories behind them: The Scelestia Room's antique Danish headboard has the face of a demon in the grain, and the bedstead in the cottage was brought in on a settler's wagon.

22830 Ferretti Rd., Groveland, CA 95321. © 866/962-6548. Fax 209/962-7750. www.yosemiterose.com. 7 rooms, including 1 suite, and 1 cottage. $135–$145 double; $165 suite; $160–$255 cottage. Rates include full breakfast. AE, DISC, MC, V. **Amenities:** Fishing, game room. *In room:* A/C, kitchen, no phone.

ALONG CALIFORNIA 140
Best Western Yosemite Way Station–Mariposa   These are typical motel accommodations—clean, comfortable, and attractive,

but nothing fancy. This is a good choice for park visitors who are seeking a comfortable bed and a hot bath for a reasonable price, and rooms are often available even during the peak weeks of summer.

4999 CA 140, Mariposa, CA. 95338 ℂ 800/528-1234 or 209/966-7545. Fax 209/966-6353. www.yosemiteresorts.us. 77 units. $79–$109 double. Rates include continental breakfast. AE, DC, DISC, MC, V. **Amenities:** Outdoor pool; whirlpool; restaurants and shops close by; public transportation into the park nearby. *In room:* A/C, TV.

Cedar Lodge
Eight miles outside of the park, this somewhat generic lodge offers large rooms with easy access to the Merced River. A nice variety makes this property an attractive option for visitors, with units ranging from standard motel-type rooms to luxurious king suites with whirlpools for two. There are also family units and rooms with kitchenettes.

9966 CA 140 (P.O. Box C), El Portal, CA 95318. ℂ 800/321-5261 or 209/379-2612. Fax 209/379-2712. www.yosemiteresorts.us. 210 units, some family units, 1 3-bedroom suite with private pool and Jacuzzi. $99–$135 double; $289–$429 suite. AE, MC, V. **Amenities:** 2 restaurants, lounge; large outdoor pool, smaller indoor pool; whirlpool; public buses to the park. *In room:* A/C, TV, rental VCRs and movies.

Highland House Bed & Breakfast
Secluded on 10 forested acres, with easy access to hiking and horseback trails that lead into the nearby Sierra National Forest, this inn is a wonderful place to relax. A mix of Cape Cod and Colonial styles of architecture, Highland House is comfortably and tastefully decorated. Common areas include the living room, with a large stone fireplace with woodstove insert, and a great den, with books and a pool table. All three rooms here have forest views; we like the Forest Retreat, with a four-poster king and a soaking tub and separate shower. The big deal, though, is breakfast, with fresh baked goods and a hot entree such as blueberry pancakes or orange French toast.

3125 Wild Dove Lane, Mariposa, CA 95338-9037. ℂ 209/966-3737. www.highlandhouseinn.com. 3 units. $95–$135 double. Rates include full breakfast. AE, MC, V. From Mariposa, head east (toward Yosemite National Park) on CA 140 for about 4 miles, turn south (right) onto Triangle Rd. for about 6 miles, and shortly after a 1-lane bridge, turn left onto Jerseydale Rd. Go 1½ miles and turn right onto Wild Dove Lane, then watch for marked driveway off to the right for the Highland House. **Amenities:** Stables. *In room:* A/C, TV/VCR.

Miners Inn
Miners Inn is a standard motel that strives to recapture the Old West. Deluxe rooms include spa tubs and fireplaces, and kitchenette units are available. There is a wine shop on-site and a small display on Bigfoot—the owner is a true believer in the big hairy fella.

CA 140 and CA 49 N., Mariposa, CA 95338. ℂ 209/742-7777. Fax 209/966-2343. 78 units. $69–$139 double; lower rates in winter. AE, DISC, MC, V. **Amenities:**

Restaurant; lounge, outdoor pool; whirlpool; public buses to Yosemite. *In room:* A/C, TV, kitchens.

Mariposa Lodge Three generations of the Gloor family have run this top-notch motel on Mariposa's main drag for over 30 years, and their standards are surprisingly high. The place has grown over the years from one building to three, with smaller (albeit reliably clean and maintained) rooms in the original structure, and larger rooms in the newer two. The suites here are not truly two-room suites, but oversize rooms with Mission decor, impressive vanities, and many private balconies. Landscaping is also superlative for a roadside motel, especially the garden courtyard around the pool. High-speed wireless Internet access (Wi-Fi) is a modern touch.

5052 CA 140 (P.O. Box 733), Mariposa, CA 95338. ℭ **800/966-8819** or 209/966-3607. Fax 209/966-5021. 45 units. $69–$99 double. AE, DISC, MC, V. **Amenities:** Outdoor pool, Jacuzzi; restaurants and shops within walking distance. *In room:* A/C, TV, fridge, microwave, coffeemaker, iron.

Poppy Hill Bed & Breakfast 🌟🌟 This restored country farmhouse, surrounded by large oak and pine trees, provides a delightful escape from the hustle and bustle of the developed areas of the park and nearby gateway communities. The inn is decorated with a variety of antiques, most from the 1800s, but also including "new" furnishings such as the 1925 Wurlitzer baby-grand piano in the parlor. (You're welcome to tickle its ivories.) Each of the three attractive rooms declares its name in its individual decor—Mariposa lily, iris, and of course, poppy—all area flowers. Rooms have queen-size beds (the Mariposa lily room also has a twin-size day bed), down comforters, bathrobes, antique furnishings, and lots of personal touches. The Mariposa lily room has a shower/tub combo; the other two rooms have large showers.

There are outside sitting areas, and a great amount of rolling lawn and flowers—one hillside bursts into color when the poppies bloom in spring. The second-floor balcony overlooks an ancient spreading oak tree, which entices the birds to entertain you while you relax in quietude. The full homemade breakfasts are extra special, with a hot entree such as eggs picante, puffed apple pancake, or croissant French toast. The entire inn is nonsmoking.

5218 Crystal Aire Dr., Mariposa, CA 95338. ℭ **800/58-POPPY** [587-6779] or 209/742-6273. www.poppyhill.com. 3 units. $120–$150 double. Rates include full breakfast. AE, DC, DISC, MC, V. Take CA 140 east out of Mariposa (toward Yosemite National Park) 3 miles, turn left on E. Whitlock Rd., travel for 1¼ miles, turn right onto Crystal Aire Dr., and go ⅛ mile to the B&B. **Amenities:** Outdoor Jacuzzi. *In room:* A/C, no phone.

Yosemite Bug Rustic Mountain Resort & Spa ✿ *Finds*   On the site of a former children's camp, the Yosemite Bug started as a hostel in 1996, but it grew and grew, and is now much, much more. The place literally has something for everybody, with accommodations that range from dorm rooms and tent-cabins to delightful private rooms, a good restaurant, a new-for-2006 spa, and loads of personality.

Situated in the forest, most of the units have woodsy, National Park–like views. The dorm rooms (single-sex, coed, or group) are basic, with bunk beds, heat, ceiling fans (no air-conditioning), individual lockable storage boxes, and conveniently located communal bathrooms. The tent-cabins have wooden floors and framing, no heat, and different bed combinations, including family units with a double and two single beds. Private rooms are themed, offering a variety of bed combinations and fun motifs ranging from modern Western to Victorian to the tie-dye-heavy "Austin Powers" room. There are handicap-accessible rooms and cabins, and a kitchen is available for those who are staying in the hostel dorm rooms. In addition, there is a computer for checking e-mail ($1 for 10 min.) as well as a Wi-Fi network in the lodge. The Yosemite Bug is along the route for the YARTS bus into Yosemite National Park ($10 round-trip). Maybe the best feature of all is the idyllic swimming hole right down the slope from the main lodge, especially on those dog days of summer.

6979 CA 140 (P.O. Box 81), Midpines, CA 95345. ✆ 866/826-7108 or 209/966-6666. Fax 209/966-9667. www.yosemitebug.com. 67 hostel beds, 20 private rooms with private bathrooms, 8 private rooms with shared bathrooms, 12 tent-cabins. Hostel beds $15–$18 per person; private room with bathroom (2–5 people) $65–$125; private room with shared bathroom (2–5 people) $40–$70; tent-cabin or walk-in campsite (2–4 people) $17–$50. DISC, MC, V. **Amenities:** Restaurant (see "Where to Eat," later in this chapter); spa; Jacuzzi; sauna; kitchen for dorm lodgers.

Yosemite View Lodge   Just outside the National Park's Arch Rock entrance, this lodge offers guests accommodations on the Merced River. Many of the rooms are brand new or recently refurbished. Many units feature fireplaces, balconies or patios, kitchenettes, and spa tubs for two.

11136 CA 140 (P.O. Box D), El Portal, CA 95318. ✆ 800/321-5261 or 209/379-2681. Fax 209/379-2704. www.yosemiteresorts.us. 335 units, some with kitchenettes. $119–$209 double; $189–$689 suite. AE, MC, V. **Amenities:** 2 restaurants, lounge; 3 outdoor pools, indoor pool; 5 outdoor whirlpools, indoor whirlpool; public buses into the park available. *In room:* A/C, TV, microwave (most rooms), refrigerator (most rooms).

ALONG CALIFORNIA 41
Château du Sureau ✿✿✿   One of the standout B&Bs in all of California (for that matter the entire U.S.), the lavish Château du

Sureau is as close as you get to Europe on the west side of the Atlantic. A world away from the rest of Oakhurst, the 9,000-square-foot inn has an elegant, near-magical ambience to it (which you pay for in spades), radiating from the villa that houses the stylish, uniquely decorated guest rooms, such as the extraordinary Saffron Room with a king-size ebony and ivory bedroom set from 1834, and the Sweet Geranium Room, with a private balcony overlooking sumptuous gardens and a canopied king. There are details both rustic (fresh fruit and fireplaces) and modern (CD players), and scads of impressive objects of art around every corner. The grounds here are similarly phenomenal—featuring a lawn-size chessboard with 3-foot-high pawns!—and the restaurant, Erna's Elderberry House, is sublime (see "Where to Eat," later in this chapter).

48688 Victoria Lane (P.O. Box 577), Oakhurst, CA 93644. © 559/683-6860. Fax 559/683-0800. www.chateausureau.com. 11 units, including a private house. $350–$550 double; $2,800 guesthouse. Rates include full breakfast. AE, MC, V. **Amenities:** Restaurant; outdoor pool; spa; bocce court. *In room:* A/C, no phones.

The Homestead ✿ Secluded on 160 acres of woodland with plenty of trails, this off-the-beaten-path establishment is a gem. The delightful cottages here are rustic yet modern, with four-poster log beds, Saltillo tile floors, stone fireplaces, and separate sitting and dining areas, plus the conveniences of TVs and air-conditioning. Each unit has its own unique bent, from the romantic Garden Cottage to the cozy Star Gazing Loft to the two-bedroom Ranch House (the only family-friendly option at this adult-oriented getaway). Kitchens are part of the package in all of the rooms; smoking is not allowed.

41110 Rd. 600, Ahwahnee, CA 93601. © 559/683-0495. Fax 559/683 8165. www.homesteadcottages.com. 5 cottages, 1 house. $145–$219 double; $349–$374 house. DISC, MC, V. 4½ miles north of Oakhurst on CA 49, then south on Rd. 600 for 2½ miles. *In room:* A/C, cable TV, kitchen, hair dryer, iron, no phone.

Hounds Tooth Inn ✿ With a Victorian look and a birth date in 1997, the Hound's Tooth is a good choice for those who want easy access to Yosemite from the south side, but want more intimacy than a motel or sprawling resort can offer. Set a few hundred feet from the highway, the off-white exterior here sheaths a dozen very similar guest rooms, each with modern conveniences of phone and TV and the flair of antique reproductions and in-room sinks. There's also a private summer house (850 sq. ft.) with a king bed and a kitchenette, plus a Jacuzzi and private patio. The garden area out back is something of a work of art, perfect for whiling away an evening in peace and quiet. Smoking is not allowed.

42971 CA 41, Oakhurst, CA 93644. ℂ **888/642-6610** or 559/642-6600. Fax 559/658-2946. www.houndstoothinn.com. 13 units, including 1 cottage. $95–$175 double; $225 cottage. AE, DC, DISC, MC, V. *In room:* A/C, cable TV/VCR, hot tubs, hair dryer, kitchenette.

Tenaya Lodge ✹   The top-rated Tenaya Lodge seems to have one foot in the Adirondack Mountains and another in the Southwest. This three- and four-story resort is on 35 acres surrounded by Sierra National Forest and features a full slate of organized recreational activities. The comfortable rooms are modern, and the grand lobby has an impressive fireplace built of river rock that towers three stories. Tenaya Lodge is an especially cozy choice for winter visitors.

1122 CA 41, Fish Camp, CA 93623. ℂ **800/635-5807** or 559/683-6555. Fax 559/683-0249. 244 units, including 20 suites. $149–$359 double; $350–$659 suite. Children stay free in parents' room. Buffet breakfast $30 per couple. AE, DC, DISC, MC, V. **Amenities:** 3 restaurants; indoor and outdoor pools; health club; game room; room service; on-site massage; general store; activity desk; seasonal sleigh or hay rides. *In room:* A/C, cable TV w/ pay movies, minibar, coffeemaker, hair dryer, iron, safe.

2 Camping

There are numerous camping opportunities both within and surrounding Yosemite National Park. Brief descriptions of individual campgrounds follow, and you'll find additional details in the campground chart in this chapter.

It's important to remember that when camping in this area, proper food storage (bear-proof canisters or lockers) is *required* for the sake of the black bears in the parks, as well as for your safety. See local bulletin boards for instructions.

INSIDE THE PARK

First, the bad news: Yosemite Valley lost half of its roughly 800 campsites during a flood in early 1997. The lost campsites will eventually be replaced somewhere outside of the Merced's floodplain, but no one knows exactly when or where this will happen. Therefore, campsite reservations are a really good idea. Reservations are accepted beginning on the 15th of each month and can be made up to 5 months in advance; make your reservations (ℂ **800/436-7275;** http://reservations.nps.gov) as soon as possible, especially for sites in the valley. Unless noted otherwise, pets are accepted in all of the following campgrounds. Additional campground information is available by touch-tone phone at ℂ 209/372-0200.

Wilderness permits are required for all overnight backpacking trips in the park, whether you decide to use an established campsite or pick out your own camping area. No wilderness camping is allowed in the valley. For more information on wilderness camping, including Yosemite's High Sierra camps, see chapter 4, "Hikes & Other Outdoor Pursuits in Yosemite."

The busiest campgrounds in the park are in Yosemite Valley. All four of the following campgrounds are in Yosemite Valley and have flush toilets and access to the showers nearby at Camp Curry ($2). Upper, Lower, and North Pines campgrounds require reservations. **Upper Pines** is pretty and shady, but you won't find peace and quiet here in the summer. Parking is available or you can take the shuttle bus to stop no. 15 or 19. **Lower Pines Campground** is wide open with lots of shade but limited privacy. Still, it's a nice place with clean bathrooms, and it's bordered on the north by a picturesque meadow. Parking is available, or take the shuttle bus to stop no. 19. **North Pines** ⊛ is beautifully situated beneath a grove of pine trees that offers lots of shade but little privacy. The campground is near the river, roughly a mile from Mirror Lake. Parking is available, or take the shuttle bus to stop no. 18. **Camp 4** (also called Sunnyside Walk-In) has tent sites only. It's a small campground that's become a magnet for hikers and climbers taking off or returning from trips. It's situated behind Yosemite Lodge, near the trailhead for Yosemite Falls, and close to rocks frequently used by novice rock climbers. Pets are not permitted. Parking is available about 50 yards away, or take the shuttle bus to stop no. 7.

Elsewhere in the park, **Bridalveil Creek Campground** at Glacier Point is set along Bridalveil Creek, which flows to Bridalveil Fall, a beauty of a waterfall, especially after a snowy winter or wet spring. Near beautiful Glacier Point, and featuring flush toilets, this campground is away from the valley crowds but within a moderate drive to the valley sights. The campground can accommodate some pack animals; call for information. Take CA 41 (from either direction) to Glacier Point Road. The campground is about 8 miles down the road.

Several campgrounds are located in the vicinity of the Big Oak Flat Entrance, roughly 20 to 25 miles from Yosemite Valley. **Hodgdon Meadow,** which has RV and tent sites, including some walk-in sites, requires reservations May through September but is first-come, first-served the rest of the year. It has flush toilets and is located about 1 mile inside the entrance along North Crane Creek and near the Tuolumne River's south fork. The Big Trees are 3 miles southeast. **Crane Flat,** a large, pleasant campground with flush toilets, is located on Big Oak Flat Road near the Tioga Road turnoff.

Tamarack Flat Campground is a bit off the beaten path and therefore more secluded than most, which means fewer folks rest their heads here. Equidistant from Yosemite Valley and Tuolumne Meadows, it has pit toilets, does not allow pets, and is not suitable for large RVs or trailers. Take Tioga Road east from Big Oak Flat Road about 3 miles and turn right onto the access road. The campground is another 3 miles down the road.

Campgrounds in the White Wolf area include **Porcupine Flat,** which offers lots of shade, shrubs, and trees, although facilities are pretty much limited to pit toilets. Located near Yosemite Creek, you have a chance of finding a spot here if you're in a pinch. Pets are not permitted. It's along Tioga Road, 16 miles west of Tuolumne Meadows and 38 miles east of Yosemite Valley. The **White Wolf Campground,** secluded in a forest, is a generally delightful campground where you might want to spend several days. It has flush toilets and offers easy access to nearby hiking, with trails that lead to several lakes, including Grant Lake and Lukens Lake. On the down side, mosquitoes make their presence felt here in summer. From Big Oak Flat Road, turn east onto Tioga Road, drive 15 miles to White Wolf Road, and turn left. The road dead-ends at the campground.

Among Yosemite's other campgrounds is **Tuolumne Meadows,** the biggest campground in the park and, amazingly, often the least crowded. Its location in the high country makes it a good spot from which to head off with a backpack. The site is also near the Tuolumne River, making it a good choice for anglers. In addition to standard RV/tent sites, the campground has 25 walk-in spaces for backpackers and eight group sites; half of the sites require reservations. There are flush toilets, and showers can be bought nearby at Tuolumne Lodge for a fee. From Big Oak Flat Road, head east on Tioga Road for about 45 miles to Tuolumne Meadows.

Wawona Campground, which requires reservations May through September (but is open year-round), has flush toilets and can accommodate pack animals; call for information. There's not much seclusion here, but the location, shaded beneath towering trees, is beautiful. The campground is near the Mariposa Grove of giant sequoias and is also close to the Merced River, which offers some of the better fishing in the park. The campground is about 1 mile north of Wawona. The **Yosemite Creek Campground** ⋐, in a pretty setting along Yosemite Creek, has pit toilets and little else in terms of facilities, but sometimes has sites available when the park's other campgrounds are full. From Big Oak Flat Road, head east on

Tioga Road for about 30 miles and turn right on the access road. The campground is 5 miles down the road.

OUTSIDE THE PARK

Yosemite is surrounded by national forests that offer campgrounds that are comparable to the ones in the park, although often less developed and less crowded. There are also private campgrounds, which usually provide level sites, complete RV hookups, hot showers, coin-operated laundries, convenience stores, and other amenities.

WEST ALONG CALIFORNIA 120

The following campgrounds, located along CA 120 west of the park, are all in the Stanislaus National Forest's **Groveland Ranger District,** 24545 CA 120, Groveland, CA 95321 (© **209/962-7825;** www.fs.fed.us/r5/stanislaus/groveland). They all have vault toilets and can accommodate rigs up to 22 feet long.

Lumsden Campground is located along the Tuolumne River, on a scenic stretch between the Hetch Hetchy and Don Pedro reservoirs. The campground offers fishing in a primitive setting but can get unbelievably hot in the summer. From Groveland, take CA 120 about 9 miles east to Ferretti Road, turn left and drive about 1 mile to Lumsden Road, turn right at Lumsden Road, and travel about 5 miles on a steep, narrow, dirt road to the campground. **Lumsden Bridge Campground** is about 1½ miles past Lumsden Campground (on Lumsden Rd.). Set in a pine and oak forest along the Tuolumne River, it is a favorite of rafters because the location is close to some of the Tuolumne River's best (and most scenic) stretches of whitewater. The **South Fork Campground,** also located along Lumsden Road, near Lumsden and Lumsden Bridge campgrounds, is a pretty spot near the Tuolumne River. It is recommended that trailers or vehicles with low ground clearance not be taken to any of the above three campgrounds.

The Pines Campground is located about 9 miles east of Groveland via CA 120, and although it's in a mixed conifer forest, it can get hot in the summer. Drinking water is available only in the summer. **Lost Claim Campground,** located about 12 miles east of Groveland via CA 120, offers easy access on a paved road. There are some trees and the river is nearby. Drinking water is supplied by a hand pump. Trailers are not recommended. Pretty **Sweetwater Campground,** located 15 miles east of Groveland on CA 120, is in a mixed conifer forest with shady sites, but it also gets hot in the summer.

Yosemite Campgrounds

Campground	Elev. (Ft.)	Total Sites	RV Hookups	Dump Station	Toilets	Drinking Water	Showers	Fire Pits/ Grills	Laundry	Public Phones	Reservations Possible	Fees	Open
Inside Yosemite National Park													
Bridalveil Creek	7,200	110	0	No	Yes	Yes	No	Yes	No	Yes	No	$12	July–Sept
Camp 4	4,000	35	0	No	Yes	Yes	Nearby	Yes	Nearby	Yes	No	$5	All year
Crane Flat	6,191	166	0	No	Yes	Yes	No	Yes	No	Yes	Yes	$18	June–Sept
Hodgdon Meadow	4,872	105	0	No	Yes	Yes	No	Yes	No	Yes	May–Sept	$18	All year
Lower Pines	4,000	60	0	Nearby	Yes	Yes	Nearby	Yes	Nearby	Yes	Yes	$18	Mar–Oct
North Pines	4,000	81	0	Nearby	Yes	Yes	Nearby	Yes	Nearby	Yes	Yes	$18	Apr–Sept
Porcupine Flat	8,100	52	0	No	Yes	No	No	Yes	No	Yes	No	$8	June–Sept
Tamarack Flat	6,315	52	0	No	Yes	No	No	Yes	No	Yes	No	$8	June–Sept
Tuolumne Meadows	8,600	304	0	Nearby	Yes	Yes	Nearby	Yes	No	Yes	Yes	$18	July–Sept
Upper Pines	4,000	238	0	Yes	Yes	Yes	Nearby	Yes	Nearby	Yes	Yes	$18	All year
Wawona	4,000	93	0	Nearby	Yes	Yes	No	Yes	No	Yes	May–Sept	$18	All year
White Wolf	8,000	74	0	No	Yes	Yes	No	Yes	No	Yes	No	$12	July–Sept
Yosemite Creek	7,659	75	0	No	Yes	No	No	Yes	No	Yes	No	$8	July–Sept

OUTSIDE THE PARK													
Lumsden	1,500	10	0	No	Yes	No	No	Yes	No	No	No	Free	All year
Lumsden Bridge	1,500	9	0	No	Yes	No	No	Yes	No	No	No	Free	Apr–Oct
Lost Claim	3,100	10	0	No	Yes	Yes	No	Yes	No	No	No	$12	May–Labor Day
The Pines	3,200	11	0	No	Yes	Yes	No	Yes	No	No	No	$12	All year
South Fork	1,500	8	0	No	Yes	No	No	Yes	No	No	No	Free	Apr–Oct
Sweetwater	3,000	12	0	No	Yes	Yes	No	Yes	No	No	No	$15	Apr–Oct
Jerseydale	4,000	8	0	No	Yes	Yes	No	Yes	No	No	No	Free	May–Nov
Summerdale	5,000	29	0	No	Yes	Yes	No	Yes	No	No	Yes	$17	June–Nov
Summit	5,800	6	0	No	Yes	No	No	Yes	No	No	No	Free	June–Oct
Big Bend	7,800	17	0	No	Yes	Yes	No	Yes	No	No	No	$15	Apr–Oct
Ellery Lake	9,500	12	0	No	Yes	Yes	No	Yes	No	No	No	$15	June–Oct
Junction	9,600	13	0	No	Yes	No	No	Yes	No	No	No	$9	June–Oct
Saddlebag Lake	10,000	20	0	No	Yes	Yes	No	Yes	No	No	No	$15	June–Oct
Tioga Lake	9,700	13	0	No	Yes	Yes	No	Yes	No	No	No	$15	June–Oct
Yosemite–Mariposa KOA	2,400	89	51	Yes	Yes	Yes	Yes	Yes	Yes	Yes	A good idea	$21–$50	All year

ALONG CALIFORNIA 140

Jerseydale Campground, located in the Sierra National Forest, 1600 Tollhouse Rd., Clovis, CA 93611-0532 (© **559/297-0706;** www.fs.fed.us/r5/sierra), is a great base for exploring the area, and provides refuge from the crowds. There are vault toilets and hiking trails, and you can get to the Merced River via a nearby trailhead. From Mariposa, drive about 12 miles northwest on CA 49 to Jerseydale Road, which leads to the campground and adjacent Jerseydale Ranger Station.

A good choice for those who want all the amenities of a top-notch commercial campground is the **Yosemite–Mariposa KOA,** 7 miles northeast of Mariposa at 6323 CA 140; mailing address P.O. Box 545, Midpines, CA 95345 (© **800/562-9391** for reservations, or 209/966-2201; www.koa.com). Located 23 miles from the park entrance, this KOA has pines and oaks that shade many of the sites, a catch-and-release fishing pond, pedal boats in the summer, a swimming pool, and a playground. There's also a convenience store and propane for sale. A kids' favorite is the train caboose containing video games. There are also a dozen camping cabins (you share the bathhouse with campers), with rates from $52 to $65.

ALONG CALIFORNIA 41

Two Sierra National Forest campgrounds (see contact information for Jerseydale Campground, above) offer pleasant camping, with vault toilets, in a woodsy atmosphere along CA 41, southwest of Yosemite. **Summerdale Campground** is about a mile north of Fish Camp via CA 41, on the south fork of the Merced River, and is often full by noon Friday; reservations are available through **www. reserveusa.com**. **Summit Campground,** in the Chowchilla Mountains, about 5 miles west of Fish Camp via a Forest Service road, is a little campground that's often overlooked.

EAST ALONG CALIFORNIA 120

The Inyo National Forest operates a number of small, attractive campgrounds along CA 120, east of the National Park. These include **Big Bend Campground,** offering flush toilets, 7 miles west of Lee Vining via CA 120. Located on the eastern Sierra along Lee Vining Creek, this campground is sparse but breathtaking. **Ellery Lake Campground,** which also has flush toilets, is at scenic Ellery Lake, about 9 miles west of Lee Vining via CA 120. **Junction Campground** is near Ellery and Tioga lakes, with easy access to the Tioga Tarns Nature Trail. It has vault toilets and is 10 miles west of Lee Vining along CA 120.

At 10,000 feet, **Saddlebag Lake Campground** is the highest-elevation drive-to campground in the state. The campground is situated along Saddlebag Lake and near Lee Vining Creek. It's beautiful and is worth staying and exploring for a while. It's also a great base for those who want to head out into the wilderness with a backpack. It has flush toilets. From Lee Vining, drive 10 miles west on CA 120, then turn north on Saddlebag Lake Road and go about 2 miles to the campground. **Tioga Lake Campground,** another high-elevation campground, is a pretty place to camp and has flush toilets. From Lee Vining, drive 10 miles west on CA 120.

Information on these U.S. Forest Service campgrounds is available from the **Mono Basin Scenic Area Visitor Center,** located on the west shore of Mono Lake (P.O. Box 429, Lee Vining, CA 93541; © **760/647-3044**), and the **Inyo National Forest,** 351 Pacu Lane, Suite 200, Bishop, CA 93514 (© **760/873-2400;** www. fs.fed.us/r5/inyo).

3 Where to Eat

There are plenty of dining possibilities in and near the park, so you certainly won't go hungry. However, you won't find many bargains, so be sure to bring a full wallet.

IN THE VALLEY

Ahwahnee Dining Room *ʀʀ* AMERICAN/INTERNATIONAL
Even if you are a dyed-in-the-wool, sleep-under-the-stars backpacker, the Ahwahnee Dining Room will not fail to make an impression. This is where the great outdoors meets four-star cuisine, and it's a wonderful place to celebrate a special occasion. The cavernous room, its candelabra chandeliers hanging from the 34-foot-high beamed ceiling, seems intimate once you're seated at a table. Don't be fooled—it actually seats 350. The menu changes frequently and offers a good variety of creative yet recognizable dishes, such as mustard-crusted sea bass, butter-braised rabbit, and filet mignon with a blue-cheese gratinée. The dinner menu includes suggested wines (from an extensive wine list) for each entree. Breakfast includes a variety of egg dishes, hotcakes, and the like, plus specialties such as a thick apple crepe filled with spiced apples and raspberry purée. Lunch choices include a grilled turkey quesadilla and grilled portobello mushrooms on a sun-dried tomato roll; and a variety of plates and salads. The dress code requires men to wear a coat and long pants in the evening; no shorts or jeans anytime.

Fun Fact Food for Thought

DNC Parks & Resorts at Yosemite reports that Yosemite visitors consume over 100,000 gallons of milk, 100,000 hot dogs, 30,000 gallons of ice cream, and 2.5 million cups of coffee annually.

The Ahwahnee, Yosemite Valley. ✆ **209/372-1489.** Dinner reservations required. Breakfast $7.50–$17; lunch $10–$14; dinner $22–$39; Sun brunch $32 adults, $17 children. AE, DC, DISC, MC, V. Mon–Sat 7–10am, 11:30am–3pm, and 5:30–9:15pm. Sun 7am–3pm and 5:30–9:15pm. Shuttle-bus stop 3.

Curry Village Coffee Corner COFFEE SHOP   Specialty coffees and fresh-baked pastries are the fare here, and you can also get ice cream after 11am.

Curry Village, Yosemite Valley. Most items $1–$4. AE, DC, DISC, MC, V. Daily 6am–10pm. Shuttle-bus stops 13A, 13B, 14, and 20.

Curry Village Pavilion *Kids* AMERICAN   A good spot for the very hungry. All-you-can-eat breakfast and dinner buffets offer a wide variety of well-prepared basic American selections at fairly reasonable prices.

Curry Village. Breakfast $9.50 adults, $7.50 children; Dinner $12 adults, $10 children. DC, DISC, MC, V. Daily 7–10am and 5:30–8pm. Shuttle-bus stops 13A, 13B, 14, and 20.

Curry Village Pizza Patio *Kids* PIZZA   Need to watch ESPN? This is the place, but you may have to wait in line. One of the park's few big screens awaits inside, and if you're a sports buff, this is the place to be. The scenic outdoor patio offers large umbrellas, table service, and a great view of Mother Nature, plus or minus a hundred kids. The lounge also taps a few brews—nothing special, but a mix aimed to please. This is a great place to chill after a long day.

Curry Village, Yosemite Valley. Pizza $8–$20. AE, DC, DISC, MC, V. Daily noon–9pm. Shuttle-bus stops 13A, 13B, 14, and 20.

Curry Village Taqueria MEXICAN   A good place for a quick bite, this taco stand offers spicy tacos, burritos, taco salads, beans, and rice.

Curry Village. $3–$6. AE, DC, DISC, MC, V. Daily 11am–5pm; Fri–Sun also 8–11am. Closed in winter. Shuttle-bus stops 13A, 13B, 14, and 20.

Degnan's Cafe AMERICAN   Adjacent to Degnan's Deli, this cafe offers specialty coffee drinks, fresh pastries, and ice cream. It's a good place for a quick bite when you're in a hurry.

Yosemite Village. Most items $1–$4. DC, DISC, MC, V. Daily 7am–7pm. Shuttle-bus stops 4 and 10.

Degnan's Deli *Value* DELI   A solid delicatessen with a large selection of generous sandwiches made to order (plus incidentals), this is our top choice for a quick, healthy lunch or supper. Sometimes the ordering line gets long, but it moves quickly. This place is half market and half deli; in addition to the made-to-order sandwiches there is a selection of prepared items—soups, salads, sandwiches, desserts, and snacks—to carry off for a day on the trail. There's also a fairly good selection of beer and wine.

Yosemite Village. $3–$8. DC, DISC, MC, V. Daily 7am–7pm. Shuttle-bus stops 4 and 10.

Degnan's Loft *Kids* ITALIAN   This cheery restaurant, with a central fireplace and high-beamed ceilings, is adjacent to Degnan's Deli and Degnan's Cafe. This is a good choice for families due to the restaurant's kid-friendly atmosphere. The menu features pizza, calzones, lasagna, salads, and desserts.

Yosemite Village. Entrees $4.25–$21. DC, DISC, MC, V. Daily noon–9pm. Shuttle-bus stops 4 and 10.

Mountain Room Restaurant AMERICAN   The best thing about this restaurant is the view. The food's excellent too, with an emphasis on local organic ingredients, but the floor-to-ceiling windows overlooking Yosemite Falls are spectacular. There's not a bad seat in the house. We suggest the grilled chicken breast, which is flavorful and moist, as are the rainbow trout amandine and the Pacific salmon. Meals come with vegetables and bread. Soup or salad is extra. There are also entrees for vegetarians and an amazing dessert tray. The Mountain Room also has a good wine list, and the Mountain Room Bar and Lounge (open 4–10pm Mon–Fri and noon–10pm Sat–Sun) has an a la carte menu available.

Yosemite Lodge. Entrees $17–$29. AE, DC, DISC, MC, V. Daily 5:30–9pm. Shuttle-bus stop 8.

Village Grill AMERICAN   The Village Grill is a fast-food joint that's a decent place to pick up a quick bite. It offers burgers, chicken sandwiches, and the like, and has outdoor seating.

Yosemite Village. Most items $3.75–$7. AE, DC, DISC, MC, V. Daily 11am–5pm. Closed in winter. Shuttle-bus stop 2.

Yosemite Lodge Food Court AMERICAN   You'll find breakfast, lunch, and dinner at this busy restaurant (serving about 2,000 meals each day), which is a vast improvement over the traditional cafeteria. It's set up with a series of food stations, where you pick up your choices before heading to the centralized cashier and then to a table inside or else the outside seating area, which features tables with umbrellas and good views of Yosemite Falls. Food stations specialize in pasta (with a choice of sauces), pizza, deli sandwiches and salads, a grill (offering burgers, hot dogs, and hot sandwiches), meat-based and vegetarian entrees, desserts and baked goods, and beverages. There's also a hot breakfast food station offering traditional American breakfast items.

Yosemite Lodge. Entrees $5–$14. AE, DC, DISC, MC, V. Daily 6:30–10am, 11:30am–2pm, and 5–8:30pm. Shuttle-bus stop 8.

ELSEWHERE IN THE PARK

Tuolumne Meadows Lodge AMERICAN   One of the two restaurants in Yosemite's high country, the lodge offers something for everyone. The breakfast menu features the basics, including eggs, pancakes, fruit, oatmeal, and granola. Dinners always include a beef, chicken, fish, pasta, and vegetarian specialty, all of which change frequently. The quality can swing, but the prime rib and New York steak are consistently good.

Tuolumne Meadows, CA 120. ✆ 209/372-8413. Reservations required for dinner. Breakfast $3.55–$6.95; dinner $8.65–$19. AE, DC, DISC, MC, V. Daily 7–9am and 6–8pm.

Wawona Hotel Dining Room ✸✸ AMERICAN   The Wawona dining room mirrors the hotel's ambience—wide open, lots of windows and sunlight. And the fare is great. For breakfast choose from a variety of items, including the Par Three, a combo of French toast or pancakes, eggs, and bacon or sausage—just what you need before hitting the golf course. Lunch features a variety of sandwiches and salads. Dinner is delectable. In addition to some exceptional entrees, such as brown sugar–rubbed pork loin with apple-onion relish and bourbon sauce, prime rib, and several seafood and veggie dishes, there are amazing appetizers. The cumin-crusted ahi, roasted whole garlic, and rock shrimp and potato risotto are sumptuous.

Wawona Hotel, Wawona Rd. ✆ 209/375-1425. Breakfast $3–$8; lunch $5–$10; dinner $14–$25. Sun buffets $9.95 breakfast, $16 brunch. AE, DC, DISC, MC, V. Mon–Sat 7:30–10am, 11:30am–1:30pm, and 5:30–9pm; Sun 7:30–10am (breakfast buffet), 10:30am–1:30pm (brunch buffet), and 5:30–9pm.

White Wolf Lodge AMERICAN   A changing menu in this casual restaurant, with a mountain lodge atmosphere, offers a variety of American standards with generous portions. Breakfast choices include eggs, pancakes, omelets, or biscuits and gravy; and dinner always includes beef, chicken, fish, pasta, and vegetarian dishes. Takeout lunches are also available from noon to 2pm.

White Wolf, Tioga Rd. © **209/372-8416.** Reservations required for dinner. Breakfast $3.85–$6.95; dinner $7–$17. AE, DC, DISC, MC, V. Daily 7:30–9:30am and 5–8:30pm.

OUTSIDE THE PARK

In addition to the following restaurants, you'll find an outlet for the reliable **Pizza Factory** chain in Mariposa at CA 140 and 5th Street (© **209/966-3112**), which offers delivery service to downtown Mariposa.

Café at the Bug 🏠🏠 (Value) AMERICAN
Ask the locals for their favorite secret place to get a great meal at a very reasonable price, and if they'll tell you, it will likely be this bustling eatery. It's a noisy, busy, somewhat self-service restaurant at the Yosemite Bug Rustic Mountain Resort & Spa, a hostel, lodge, and campground 10 miles from Mariposa on the way to Yosemite National Park. This casual restaurant contains several rooms with knotty-pine walls, hardwood floors, wooden chairs, Formica tables, and an open-beamed ceiling that features suspended skis and a kayak. There are a woodstove, some games, and couches where lodgers lounge. You order at a counter and your food is delivered to your table.

The food is great: innovative American dishes with Mediterranean and Californian influences. Although the dinner menu changes nightly, popular entrees include top sirloin and a citrus glazed broiled chicken breast. You also might have a trout filet with lime butter, or stuffed portobello mushrooms. (There is at least one vegetarian and one vegan option at every meal.) Breakfasts here range from bacon and eggs to buckwheat pancakes or granola; and lunches, available from 7am to 3pm, include a variety of sandwiches prepared as sack lunches for those heading out into the park.

At the Yosemite Bug Rustic Mountain Resort & Spa, 6979 CA 140, Midpines. © **209/966-6666.** Breakfast and lunch items $4.50–$6.50; dinner entrees $7–$13. DISC, MC, V. Daily 7am–9pm.

Castillo's Mexican Food MEXICAN
Established in 1955, this cheerful, cozy cantina serves generous portions of well-prepared Mexican favorites. Entrees come with salad, rice, and beans, and can also be ordered a la carte. A house specialty, the *tostada compuesta,* fills a hungry belly with your choice of meat, plus beans, lettuce, and cheese, stuffed into a bowl-shaped crisp flour tortilla and topped with avocado dip and sour cream. A variety of Mexican combo plates are served, and you can also choose several steak specialties or seafood

dishes such as jumbo shrimp fajitas. For those who like their hot food with extra fire, there's *camarones a la diabla*—shrimp sautéed in butter, garlic, and crushed red chile peppers. The outdoor seating in a garden area is our favorite spot here.

4995 5th St., Mariposa. © 209/742-4413. Reservations recommended in summer. Lunch entrees $6–$11; dinner entrees $8–$15. AE, DISC, MC, V. Mon–Thurs 11am–9pm; Fri–Sat 11am–9:30pm. Closed Sun. Closes 1 hr. earlier in winter.

Charles Street Dinner House ☆☆☆ AMERICAN Locally famous for its charbroiled steaks (marinated and herb-crusted filet mignon and New York steak, 10 oz. each), the Charles Street Dinner House has been the locals' choice for fresh seafood and a variety of other specialties for more than 25 years. We especially recommend the New Zealand rack of lamb, broiled, with mint glaze; and the broiled Peking breast of duck, served with orange sauce. Or try the scallone—abalone and scallops sautéed with lemon butter and toasted almonds. The restaurant is located in a historic building from the 1800s, and decor is straight out of the Old West, with a huge wagon wheel in the front window and touches that include family photos and fresh flowers. Service is excellent.

5043 Charles St., Mariposa. © **209/966-2366**. Reservations recommended. Entrees $12–$40. AE, DISC, MC, V. Tues–Sat 5–9pm, Sun 9am–2pm and 5–9pm.

Erna's Elderberry House ☆☆☆ EUROPEAN/CALIFORNIAN One of the most renowned eateries in the Yosemite area, this elegant restaurant at Château du Sureau is a feast for the eyes, with a contemporary seating area with purple walls and modern prints adjoining a more traditionally elegant room. Likewise, it is a feast for the taste buds, with a nightly changing menu that might include any number of European culinary traditions sculpted into a meal that is definitively Californian. Offerings might range from marinated mussels and chilled carrot-coconut soup to red pepper and prosciutto barded beef tenderloin, spinach gnocchi, and blueberry-yogurt terrine. Each menu comes with a list of recommended wines. Proprietor Erna Kubin-Clanin and company also offer regular gourmet cooking classes here.

48688 Victoria Lane (at Château du Sureau), Oakhurst. © 559/683-6800. Reservations recommended. Prix-fixe dinners $85, prix-fixe brunch $38. AE, DISC, MC, V. Daily 5:30–8:30pm; Sun also 11am–1pm.

Groveland Hotel's Victorian Room ☆☆ CALIFORNIAN Top-notch food in a casual atmosphere is what you'll experience at this fine restaurant. The menu has something for everyone and is constantly changing to reflect what's fresh and in season. There's a sumptuous rack of lamb marinated in rosemary and garlic, salmon with fresh cucumber and dill, chicken breast with fresh-fruit salsa, and more. The menu usually has fresh seafood and pasta specials, as well as an innkeeper's special. All entrees are served with soup or salad and fresh, warm bread. The *Wine Spectator* award-winning wine list—wine being one of owner Peggy Mosley's passions—is fantastic, and in summer there is also courtyard dining.

18767 CA 120, Groveland. 🕐 **800/273-3314** or 209/962-4000. Fax 209/962-6674. Reservations suggested in summer. Entrees $16–$30. AE, DC, DISC, MC, V. Daily 6–9pm in summer and 6–8pm in winter.

Happy Burger Diner 🕊 *Finds* AMERICAN   One of the best fast-food joints we've seen anywhere, the Happy Burger offers practically any type of fast food you can think of—it has the region's largest menu—with everything cooked fresh to order. The food here takes a few minutes longer than at your usual chain fast-food restaurants, but it's worth it. Breakfasts (served until 11am) include numerous egg dishes, French toast, pancakes, oatmeal, and the like. The lunch and dinner menu, served all day, features a multitude of charbroiled burgers, sandwiches, stuffed potatoes, Mexican dishes, salads, and dinner plates such as top sirloin and fried shrimp.

In typical fast-food style, you order your food at the counter; then sit at booths, among the record album covers from the 1960s and '70s and a vintage pinball game, where your piping-hot food is delivered an instant later.

5120 CA 140 (at 12th St.), Mariposa. 🕐 **209/966-2719.** Menu items $3–$15. AE, DISC, MC, V. Daily 6am–9pm.

Iron Door Saloon and Grill 🕊 AMERICAN   In 1852, this establishment started serving whiskey from an "'obligatory' plank over two flour barrels," making it California's oldest bar. Now it's the colorful anchor to a city block of businesses (including a soda fountain, an art gallery, and a general store), with scads of dollar bills hanging from the ceiling alongside rusted mining equipment, a menagerie of taxidermy, and odd little displays on such topics as the origin of Groveland's name and the career of Black Bart. The menu is fairly basic, with steaks and burgers and poultry as well as fresh fish and pasta. You can eat in the 150-year-old bar or the adjacent dining room, which is more upscale with tiled floors, rock walls, and historic photographs. Lunch features wraps and salads (and floats and shakes from the soda fountain). While not bad, the food and service don't quite live up to the colorful atmosphere, but the Iron Door is a can't-miss nonetheless.

18761 CA 120, Groveland. ✆ **209/962-6244.** Lunch entrees $7–$9, dinner entrees $10–$23. MC, V. Mon–Thurs 11am–9pm; Fri–Sat 11am–10pm. Bar open later.

PJ's Cafe and Pizzeria PIZZA/SANDWICHES   Best known as a pizzeria and burger house, PJ's serves a hearty breakfast with an eye toward good health. That being said, you can still order bacon and eggs without getting the evil eye. For lunch, the taco and Cobb salads are especially tasty. The battered cod is also quite good. We like the pizzas, too, which range from create-your-own to a yummy pesto-artichoke-tomato combination; and prime rib is featured on weekends.

18986 CA 120, Groveland. ✆ **209/962-7501.** Entrees $3–$8; pizza $5–$17. No credit cards. Daily 7am–8pm.

Savoury's ✸✸ INTERNATIONAL FUSION   In the Art Deco confines of a former California Highway Patrol office, this eatery quickly won the hearts of locals after opening in spring 2003. Not surprising, since proprietor-chef Mirriam Wackerman had catered in the area for years, and customers often urged her to follow her dreams and open a restaurant. Now that she has, the results are top-notch, with a menu of simple, fresh dishes that meld culinary traditions near and far: jambalaya linguini, chipotle pesto chicken, grilled lemon-chive scallops, and the only flat-iron steak in town, Cajun-spiced and pan-seared. For dessert, bite into a decadent dish of panna cotta, the Italian equivalent of crème brûlée on a bed of strawberry sauce. There is a cozy but sleek main dining room, as well as a delightful vine-clad patio, sandwiched between historic redbricks, out back.

5027 CA 140, Mariposa. ✆ **209/966-7677.** Entrees $11–$23. AE, DISC, MC, V. Tues–Sat 5–9:30pm.

PICNIC & CAMPING SUPPLIES

If you forget something, chances are you'll be able to get it in the park in bustling Yosemite Valley, but elsewhere in the park it's tough to find equipment. The best place to get supplies and camping equipment in the valley is the **Yosemite Village Store,** which stocks groceries, film, and maps, and has an ATM. Nearby, the **Village Sport Shop** has fishing, camping, and other outdoor gear, plus it sells fishing licenses. The **Yosemite Lodge Gift Shop** and **Curry Village General Store** stock some supplies. The **Curry Village Mountain Shop** sells clothing and equipment for day hikes as well as backcountry excursions, and the **Tuolumne Meadows Gift & Mountain Shop** also carries backpacking supplies, including maps and dehydrated food. The **Badger Pass Sport Shop** (open only during the snow season) stocks ski clothing and other winter supplies. There are also several small convenience stores located throughout the park.

In **Mariposa** you'll find a good selection of groceries plus a deli at **Pioneer Market,** at 5034 Coakley Circle, behind the town rest area (© **209/742-6100**). Our choice for a grocery store in **Oakhurst** is **Raley's** at 40041 CA 41 (© **559/683-8300**). Just outside the park's **El Portal** Entrance, on CA 140, is the well-stocked **El Portal Food Market** (© **209/379-2632**). For a better selection (and better prices) you can stop at the **major supermarket and discount chains** in **Merced** or **Fresno,** the largest cities in the park vicinity.

6

Exploring Sequoia & Kings Canyon

Most of the land in these parks is wilderness, best explored on foot. There are few roads. The three main access points enter the park from the southwest, and much of Sequoia & Kings Canyon remains undeveloped. The National Park Service and many visitors prefer it that way. Here the park's guardians are determined to protect their charge from the hazards of excessive popularity. If you visit here after staying in Yosemite, Grand Canyon, or other big-name national parks, be prepared for a shock. There are no shuttle buses with tour guides pointing out landmarks, few scheduled events, and a definite lack of attractions except for the real reason for the existence of these parks—the beauty and majesty of some of the largest living things on earth. This is nature, and none of this is likely to change anytime soon. You can expect far fewer people, far less prepackaged entertainment, and lots more to explore at your leisure.

1 Essentials

ACCESS/ENTRY POINTS

You'll find the Big Stump Entrance (Kings Canyon National Park) via CA 180, and the Ash Mountain Entrance (Sequoia National Park) via CA 198, both from the west. Continuing east on CA 180 also brings you to an entrance near Cedar Grove Village in the canyon itself, which is open only in summer. See the map in chapter 2 for general highway-access information. To access the Mineral King area of Sequoia National Park, take the steep, twisting Mineral King Road (closed in winter) off of CA 198, just a few miles outside the Ash Mountain Entrance.

VISITOR CENTERS & INFORMATION

The parks have three major visitor centers open year-round, some seasonal facilities, and a museum, where you can buy books and maps and discuss your plans with park rangers. In Sequoia National

---

⟨Tips⟩ Marmot Invasion

Always do a quick check under your hood before leaving a parking lot. Marmots, especially in the Mineral King area, love munching on car hoses and wiring, leaving a trail of disabled vehicles in their wake. A good number of them have stowed away in a car's engine compartment and hitched rides with unsuspecting drivers to other parts of the parks; several have ridden as far as the Los Angeles area!

Park, the largest visitor center is **Foothills Visitor Center** (© 559/565-3135), just inside the Ash Mountain Entrance on CA 198. Exhibits focus on the Sierra foothills, a biologically diverse ecosystem. The **Giant Forest Museum** (© 559/565-4480) is housed in a historic building and offers extensive exhibits on giant sequoias. **Lodgepole Visitor Center** (© 559/565-4436) includes exhibits on geology, wildlife, air quality, and park history. It's located 4½ miles north of Giant Forest Village, and is closed Tuesday through Thursday in winter. The **Kings Canyon Visitor Center** in Grant Grove, Kings Canyon National Park (© 559/565-4307), includes exhibits on logging and the role of fire in the forests. Open summers only is a small visitor center at **Cedar Grove** in Kings Canyon and a ranger station at Sequoia's **Mineral King,** where you can get backcountry permits and information.

FEES

It costs $20 per motor vehicle ($10 per individual on foot, bike, or motorcycle) to enter the park for up to 7 days. Camping fees range from $12 to $20 a night to camp in the park. The Sequoia & Kings Canyon yearly pass, which allows unlimited entry into the park but does not cover camping fees, sells for $40.

Also see "Passes & Permits You Can Get in Advance," in chapter 2.

REGULATIONS & WARNINGS

In Sequoia & Kings Canyon, there is a 14-day camping limit from June 14 to September 14, with a maximum of 30 camping days per year. Check campsite bulletin boards for additional regulations. Some campgrounds close in winter (see chart in chapter 8). Pets are allowed in campgrounds, but they must be on a leash and are not allowed on any trails.

The most important warning in Sequoia & Kings Canyon, which cannot be repeated too often, is that this is **bear country,** and proper food storage is required for the safety and health of both visitors and the resident black bears. In addition, rattlesnakes are common, so be careful where you put your feet and hands. In the foothills, check your clothes frequently for ticks; poison oak is another hazard. The roads in the park are particularly steep and winding. Those in RVs will find it easiest to come by way of CA 180 from Fresno.

FAST FACTS: Sequoia & Kings Canyon National Parks

ATMs You'll find bank machines at most of the commercial areas in the park, including Grant Grove (in the lobby between the gift shop and restaurant), at Lodgepole Market, and at the Cedar Grove Market (summer only).

Car Trouble/Towing Services In Sequoia only, call AAA (© 559/565-4070) 24 hours a day for jump starts, gas, and minor repairs. For a tow in either park, call © 559/565-3341, then press 0.

Climate See "When to Go," in chapter 2.

Emergencies Call © 911.

Gas Stations There are no gas stations in Sequoia & Kings Canyon National Parks. Cans of emergency gas are sold in park stores, and there are gas stations at the Kings Canyon Lodge in Giant Sequoia National Monument, between Grant Grove and Cedar Grove, Stony Creek Lodge, between Grant Grove and Wuksachi, and at Hume Lake. However, gasoline prices are notably lower in the nearby towns of Three Rivers and Visalia on CA 198, or in the Fresno area along CA 180.

Laundromats You'll find a laundry at the Lodgepole Market Center in Sequoia National Park, and at Cedar Grove Village in Kings Canyon.

Maps General maps are handed out at park entrances. These are useful in planning your drive through the parks. Many of the shorter trails are well marked, but when planning major hikes or exploring the backcountry, pick up a topographical map at a visitor center or ranger station. Excellent pocket maps, available throughout the parks for about $3 each, highlight main features and trails for selected areas of the parks, including Cedar Grove, Giant Forest, Mineral King, Grant Grove, and Lodgepole.

Medical Services The nearest medical facilities are located in the gateway towns of Fresno, Visalia, and Three Rivers.

Permits Required for all overnight camping in the backcountry (see chapter 7, "Hikes & Other Outdoor Pursuits in Sequoia & Kings Canyon"). In Sequoia & Kings Canyon, call © 559/565-3766. Information is also available online at **www.nps.gov/seki/bcinfo.htm**.

Post Offices There is a post office at Lodgepole Village in Sequoia National Park and at Grant Grove Village in Kings Canyon.

Supplies In Sequoia, the widest selection can be found at the Lodgepole Market Center, open summer only. Smaller markets with food and supplies are located at Grant Grove and Cedar Grove. In winter, a small selection of supplies is available at the store in Wuksachi Lodge. There are also stores in Three Rivers and Visalia (see "For Picnic & Camping Supplies," in chapter 8).

Weather & Road Conditions Call the National Park Service information line (© 559/565-3341) and follow instructions.

2 Orientation

The parks are roughly equidistant (5 hr. by car) from both San Francisco and Los Angeles. Kings Canyon National Park bounds Sequoia National Park on the north and is nearest to Yosemite and Fresno. Kings Canyon has the developed areas of Grant Grove and Cedar Grove. In Sequoia, you'll find the Giant Forest sequoia grove, as well as Lodgepole, the Foothills, and Mineral King. The main entrance (for all except Mineral King) is on CA 198, via Ash Mountain through Visalia and Three Rivers. From Sequoia's boundary, Visalia is 36 miles and Three Rivers is 7 miles. Although it's impossible to drive through the parks from west to east—the High Sierras get in the way—a north–south road, the Generals Highway, connects Grant Grove in Kings Canyon National Park with Giant Forest in Sequoia National Park. The highway runs 25 miles between two giant sequoias named for famous American generals—the General Grant Tree and the General Sherman Tree. Allow at least an hour to drive between the two on this slow, winding route. From several miles inside the Ash Mountain Entrance to Giant Forest, the Generals Highway is narrow and winding and not recommended for vehicles over 22 feet long, which should enter the parks from CA

180. The road to Mineral King turns south off CA 198 about 3 miles east of Three Rivers, crosses private and public land, and heads 11 miles to the Lookout Point Entrance. From here it's another 15 miles to Mineral King. This steep, narrow, twisting dead-end road is closed in winter and does not reconnect with any other park roadways, which puts the Mineral King area off-limits to motor vehicles during the winter and well into spring.

INTRODUCING SEQUOIA NATIONAL PARK

The best-known stand of sequoias in the world can be found in **Giant Forest,** part of Sequoia National Park. Named in 1875 by explorer and environmentalist John Muir, this area consists mostly of huge meadows and a large grove of trees. At the northern edge of the grove, you can't miss the General Sherman Tree, considered the largest living tree on the planet, although it is neither the tallest nor widest. Its size is noteworthy because of the tree's mass—experts estimate the weight of its trunk at about 1,385 tons. It is believed to be about 2,100 years old, *and it's still growing.* The General Sherman Tree is 275 feet tall, measures 102½ feet around at its base, and its largest branch measures 6¾ feet in diameter. Every year, it adds enough new wood to make another 60-foot-tall tree. The tree is part of the 2-mile Congress Trail, a foot trail that includes groups of trees with names such as the Senate and the House. Also in the area is the **Beetle Rock Education Center,** a fun place for kids to investigate science and nature.

Another interesting stop in Giant Forest is **Tharp's Log,** a cabin named after the first non–Native American settler in the area, Hale Tharp, who grazed cattle among the giant sequoias and built a

---

Fun Fact A Question of Size

Until recently, the National Park Service has claimed that the General Sherman Tree is the largest living thing on earth. Technically, however, this may not be quite true, and now the claim is that it is the largest living tree, still quite a distinction. The reason for the change? Park officials say it has been discovered that there may be some underground fungi that are actually bigger than the General Sherman Tree. In addition, there are groves of aspen trees, which share a common root system and, therefore, may be considered one living thing, thereby exceeding the General in overall size.

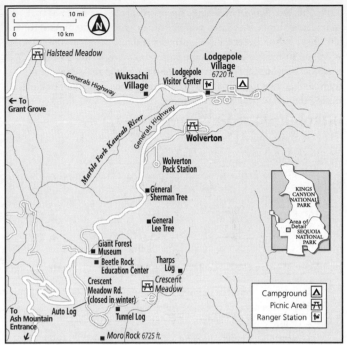

summer cabin in the 1860s from a fallen sequoia hollowed by fire. It is the oldest cabin remaining in the park.

Pretty **Crescent Meadow** is a pristine clearing dotted with wildflowers and tall grasses. A trail (described in "The Highlights," later in this chapter) wraps around the meadow. This is also the trail head for several backcountry hikes.

Also in the area is **Moro Rock,** a large granite dome well worth the half-hour climb up and back. From the top, Moro Rock offers one of the most spectacular views of the dark and barren Great Western Divide, which includes the Kaweah Range. The divide is one of two crests in the southern Sierra Nevada, but is not officially the main crest, which lies to the east and is obscured from view.

Lodgepole, the most developed area in both parks, lies just northeast of Giant Forest on the Generals Highway. Here you'll find the largest visitor center in the parks, plus a large market, several places to eat, a laundry, a post office, and showers.

Nearby, the **Wuksachi Village** has replaced the old facilities that were damaging to the Giant Forest sequoia grove. A dining room, gift shop, and lodge have all recently opened.

About 16 miles south of Giant Forest are the **Foothills.** Located near the Ash Mountain Entrance, the Foothills possesses a visitor center, several campgrounds, a picnic area, and Hospital Rock, a large boulder with ancient pictographs believed to have been painted by the Monache Indians who once lived here. Nearby are about 50 grinding spots probably used to smash acorns into flour. A short trail leads down to a serene place along the Kaweah River where the water gushes over rapids into deep, clear pools.

Located in the southern part of the park, **Mineral King** is a pristine high-mountain valley carved by glaciers and bordered by the tall peaks of the Great Western Divide. Red and orange shales mix with white marble, black metamorphic shale, and granite to give the rocky landscape a rainbow of hues. This area resembles the Rocky Mountains more than the rest of the Sierra Nevada because the peaks are formed of metamorphic rock. A silver prospector gave Mineral King its name in the 1800s, and the region was annexed to the park in 1978. The trails in Mineral King begin at 7,500 feet and climb. Park rangers conduct hikes on summer weekends. To reach the area, head west from the Ash Mountain Entrance 3 miles on CA 198 to the turnoff—watch for the sign. Then it's a 28-mile trip that makes 698 tight turns and takes 1½ hours. Trailers, RVs, and buses are not allowed. The road is closed in winter, when the area is prone to avalanches.

INTRODUCING KINGS CANYON NATIONAL PARK

With its rugged canyon, huge river, and desolate backcountry, Kings Canyon is considered a hiker's dream. Kings Canyon comprises Grant Grove and Cedar Grove, as well as portions of the Monarch Wilderness and Jennie Lakes Wilderness. *Note:* Between Grant Grove and Cedar Grove is Giant Sequoia National Monument, which is managed as part of Sequoia National Forest. This region includes Hume Lake, Boyden Cavern, and several campgrounds.

Grant Grove is the most crowded region in either park. Here you'll find the towering General Grant Tree amid a grove of spectacular giant sequoias. The tree was discovered by Joseph Hardin Tomas in 1862, and named 5 years later by Lucretia P. Baker to honor Ulysses S. Grant. The tree measures 267½ feet tall and 107½ feet around, and is thought to be the world's third largest living tree, possibly 2,000 years old (just a youngster in this neighborhood!).

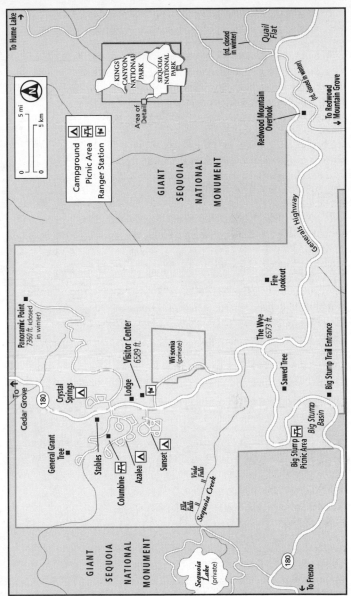

Cedar Grove

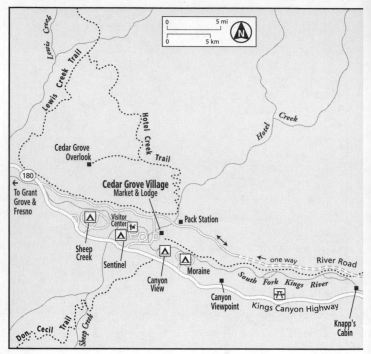

The tree was officially declared the "Nation's Christmas Tree," by President Calvin Coolidge in 1926, and is the centerpiece of an annual Christmas tree ceremony.

Two and a half miles southwest of the grove is the Big Stump Trail, an instructive hike that can be slightly depressing as it winds among the remains of logged sequoias. Since sequoia wood decays slowly, you'll see century-old piles of leftover sawdust that remain from the logging days. In summer, visitors can drive a short distance to Panoramic Point, stand atop this 7,520-foot ledge, and look across a long stretch of the Sierra Nevada for a glimpse of Kings Canyon.

Although in the same park, **Cedar Grove** seems a world away. That this region is around today is sheer luck. There were plans to flood Kings Canyon by damming the Kings River, a decision that would have buried Cedar Grove beneath a deep lake. Today that is considered an incomprehensible move. With the flood threat abated, the region stood to become another Yosemite, but people

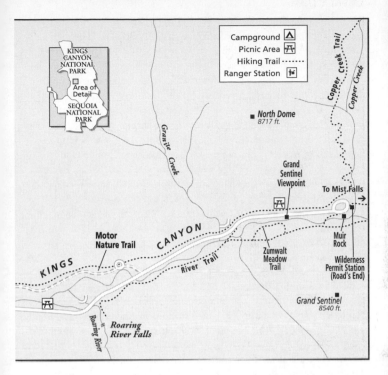

fought hard to avoid the overcrowding and development that had occurred in Yosemite, and eventually everyone agreed that there were better uses for the Sierras than to convert it into a giant parking garage. It was finally annexed in 1965, and, under a master plan for the area, will remain as it is today.

Cedar Grove is covered with lush foliage, crashing waterfalls, and miles upon miles of solitude. Half the fun is driving through Kings Canyon as its sheer granite walls close around you and the wild South Fork of the Kings River tumbles by. One mile east of the Cedar Grove Village turnoff is Canyon View, where visitors can see the glacially carved U-shape of Kings Canyon. Easily accessible nature trails in Cedar Grove include Zumwalt Meadow, Roaring River Falls, and Knapp's Cabin. **Zumwalt Meadow** is dotted with ponderosa pine and has good views of two rock formations: Grand Sentinel and North Dome. The top of Grand Sentinel is 8,504 feet above sea level, while North Dome, which some say resembles Half

Dome in Yosemite, tops out at 8,717 feet. The mile-long trail around the meadow is one of the prettiest in the park. The best place to access this walk is at a parking lot 4½ miles east of the turnoff for Cedar Grove Village.

Roaring River Falls is a 5-minute walk from the parking area, 3 miles east of the turnoff to Cedar Grove Village. Even during summer and dry years, water crashes through a narrow granite chute into a cold green pool below. During a wet spring, these falls are powerful enough to drench visitors who venture too close. **Knapp's Cabin** can be reached via a short walk from a turnoff 2 miles east of the road to Cedar Grove Village. Here, during the 1920s, Santa Barbara businessman George Knapp commissioned lavish fishing expeditions and used this tiny cabin to store his expensive gear.

Cedar Grove also hosts a small village with a store and gift shop, restaurant, laundry, showers, lodge, and campgrounds. This region of the park is often less crowded than others. Remember that it is also closed from mid-November to mid-April.

The **Monarch Wilderness** is a 45,000-acre region protected under the 1984 California Wilderness Act. Part of it lies on the grounds of Sequoia National Forest, adjoining the wilderness in Kings Canyon National Park. It's tough to reach, and so steep that hikers practically need to be roped in to climb. You're close to the wilderness area when you pass Kings Canyon Lodge and Boyden Cavern.

The **Jennie Lakes Wilderness** is even smaller at 10,500 acres. Although tiny enough to hike through in a day, it exhibits a variety of wilderness features, including the 10,365-foot Mitchell Peak and several wide lowland meadows. This region lies between the Generals Highway and CA 180, east of Grant Grove. About 7 miles southeast of Grant Grove, Big Meadows Road (closed in winter) takes off from Generals Highway and heads east into Sequoia National Forest. From this road you can access several trails that lead into Jennie Lakes Wilderness.

3 The Highlights

The view atop **Moro Rock** is one of the most spectacular in the Sierra—the Great Western Divide dominates the eastern horizon. These high-elevation, barren mountains can appear dark and ominous, even though snow caps the ridgeline throughout the year. The cliffs appear towering and steep, and with some peaks over 13,000 feet, they are only slightly below the summit of Mount Whitney (14,474 ft.), which is obscured from view. The climb to the top of

A New National Monument Is Created

Some of the most beautiful scenery in the Sequoia & Kings Canyon National Parks area is not actually in either of these national parks, but in an adjacent section of the Sequoia National Forest that was recently designated a national monument.

Covering 328,000 acres, Giant Sequoia National Monument was created by proclamation by President Bill Clinton on April 15, 2000. The monument contains 38 groves of sequoias, including some of the most magnificent giant trees to be seen anywhere. In addition, it has towering domes of granite; scenic Hume Lake, a popular destination for boaters and anglers; and the spectacular Kings Canyon—the deepest canyon in North America, with elevations ranging from 1,000 to 11,000 feet.

Among the hiking trails in the monument is the Boole Tree Trail, a moderate 2.5-mile loop trail that leads to Boole Tree, the largest sequoia in the 1.1-million-acre Sequoia National Forest, and the eighth largest tree in the world. This trail, located off Forest Road 13S55 off Kings Canyon Highway, includes forest and open country, where you'll see sequoias, scenic vistas of the Kings River, and wildflowers in summer.

An easy walk on the quarter-mile (each way) **Chicago Stump Trail** leads to the stump of the General Noble Tree, which was cut down, cut into pieces, and then reassembled and displayed at the 1893 World's Fair in Chicago. Some fairgoers refused to believe that a tree could grow so big, and dubbed it "the California hoax."

Information about other attractions and facilities within the monument, such as the beautiful drive through Kings Canyon and the underground world of Boyden Cave, are discussed elsewhere in this book. For additional information on Giant Sequoia National Monument, contact the **Hume Lake Ranger District,** Sequoia National Forest, 35860 E. Kings Canyon Rd. (CA 180), Dunlap, CA 93621 (© **559/338-2251;** www.r5.fs.fed.us/sequoia).

the Rock takes visitors up hundreds of stairs, so pace yourself. The summit offers a narrow, fenced plateau with endless views. During a full moon, the mountain peaks shimmer like silver. See "Seeing the Parks by Car," below.

Mist Falls is a wide, powerful waterfall accessible only on foot (see chapter 7), but the trek is well worth the effort. The waterfall is especially impressive during spring and early summer, when it's fed by snowmelt, and the cascading water crashing onto the rocks below drowns out most other sounds. This is also when you're likely to see rainbows galore.

Crescent Meadow is a large, picturesque clearing dotted with high grass and wildflowers, and encircled by a forest of firs and sequoias. The park's oldest cabin is along this route as well. This is a particularly nice hike in early morning and at dusk, when the indirect sunlight allows for the best photography (see chapter 7).

4 Go Inside the Earth in Two Caves

Although there are more than 200 caves in this area, only two are open for tours by the general public—one in Sequoia National Park and the other in Giant Sequoia National Monument, just outside Kings Canyon National Park.

South of the Giant Forest in Sequoia National Park is the turnoff from CA 198 for **Crystal Cave,** a beautiful underground world that was formed from limestone turned to marble. The cave contains an array of cave formations, many still growing, that range from sharply pointed stalactites and towering stalagmites to elaborate flowing draperies. To reach the entrance, drive 7 miles down the narrow winding road (RVs, trailers, and buses are prohibited), and walk a half-mile down a steep path to the cave. *Note:* To take a tour, you need to get tickets in advance at either the Lodgepole or Foothills visitor centers. Tickets are not sold at the cave.

The Sequoia Natural History Association conducts **45-minute guided tours** along paved, lighted pathways. The tours are offered from mid-June to Labor Day daily every half-hour from 11am to

---

Impressions

It is in this cave [Crystal Cave] that nature has lavishly traced her design in decorative glory.
                              —Park superintendent Walter Fry, 1925

4pm, from mid-May to mid-June and after Labor Day to late September Friday through Monday on the hour from 11am to 4pm (10am–4pm every ½-hr. on Memorial Day weekend). The cost is $10 for adults, $8 for seniors 62 and older, and $5 for children 6 to 12; admission is free for children under 6. A special **discovery tour** is offered in summer, Sunday through Friday at 4:15pm. It is less-structured, limited to 12 people, has a minimum age requirement of 13, and a fee of $16 per person. The cave is a constant 48°F (9°C), so take a sweater or jacket. Sturdy footwear is recommended, and strollers, tripods, and backpacks are prohibited. Information is available at visitor centers or by telephone (© **559/565-3759**).

Ten miles west of Cedar Grove, in Giant Sequoia National Monument, is **Boyden Cavern,** the only other cave in the area that hosts tours. Boyden is an especially scenic cave, known for a wide variety of formations including rare "shields," which consist of two roughly circular halves that look like flattened clam shells. Highlights include a flowstone formation known as Mother Nature's Wedding Cake, and the appropriately named Christmas Tree and Baby Elephant formations. The cave is open daily April through October. Hours are 11am to 4pm in April, May, and October; and 10am to 5pm June through September. Visitors see the cave on guided 45-minute tours that follow a well-lighted, handrail-equipped trail. Tours leave approximately every hour on the hour. The cost is $10 for ages 14 and up, $5 for children 3 to 13; admission is free for children 2 and younger. Reservations are not required. Special flashlight tours (bring your own flashlight) are also available, by reservation only, Friday and Saturday evenings, at the same prices as regular tours. For information, contact **Sierra Nevada Recreation Corporation,** P.O. Box 78, Vallecito, CA 95251 (© **866/762-2837** or 209/736-2708; www.caverntours.com).

5 How to See the Parks in 1 or 2 Days

Eighty percent of the parks' visitors come here on day trips—an amazing statistic considering the geography of this place. Three to four days will do the parks justice, but it is possible to take a short walk through a grove of big trees in one afternoon. Day-trippers should stick to Grant Grove if possible—it's the most accessible. Coming from the south, Giant Forest is a good alternative, although the trip takes a while on the steep and narrow Generals Highway. Cedar Grove and Mineral King, two other destination points, are farther afield and require an early start or an overnight stay.

If you have only 1 day, we recommend driving from the foothills through Giant Forest to Grant Grove, or vice versa. It's about 2 hours through the park, plus whatever additional time is necessary to resume your route outside its entrances. Start at a park visitor center—there's one near each location and it's a good place to get your bearings. Whether traveling from the north or south, you'll see the varied terrain within the park as you pass through dense forest, exposed meadows, and scrubby foothills covered in oaks and underbrush. In spring and summer, much of the route may be dotted by wildflowers. The southern portion runs along the Kaweah River. This route also passes two large stands of giant sequoias: one at Grant Grove and the other at Giant Forest. Both have easy trails looping through the majestic stands. At Grant Grove, a footpath passes lengthwise through a fallen sequoia.

6 Seeing the Parks by Car

Although these two parks are generally considered the domain of hikers and have only 127 miles of paved roads between them, you will have a use for your car here. Those not willing or physically able to lace up a pair of hiking boots and take off down a trail will be able to enjoy the scenery, often from the comfort of their motor vehicles or from roadside and near-roadside viewpoints.

The **Generals Highway** runs almost 50 miles from Sequoia National Park's Ash Mountain Entrance to Grant Grove in Kings Canyon National Park, passing through the Giant Forest, where you'll see the world's largest sequoia trees. It's a very pretty drive, and you can stop to see the Giant Forest Museum and the General Sherman Tree. There are also several easy walking trails along the way (see chapter 7). From several miles inside the Ash Mountain Entrance to Giant Forest, Generals Highway is narrow and winding and not recommended for vehicles over 22 feet long.

For a short, scenic drive in Sequoia National Park we recommend the paved **Moro Rock/Crescent Meadow Road,** a 3-mile dead-end road (open in summer only) that runs from the Giant Forest Museum, along the Generals Highway, south and east through a grove of sequoias. Along the way you can see the fallen sequoia at Auto Log (now too rotted to support a vehicle), drive through a hollowed-out fallen sequoia at Tunnel Log, and stop for a steep quarter-mile walk up to the top of Moro Rock for a spectacular panoramic view. This road ends at Crescent Meadow, known for its colorful wildflowers in summer. See also the sections on Moro Rock and Crescent Meadow in "The Highlights," above.

Kings Canyon Highway, from the Grant Grove area to Cedar Grove in Kings Canyon National Park, is a lovely drive of some 35 miles, but most of the especially scenic sections of this drive are not in the park. Instead, some of the best roadside scenery is in Giant Sequoia National Monument (see the box earlier in this chapter). Kings Canyon Highway (also called CA 180) is high above the Kings River for part of its journey, offering breathtaking vistas of the canyon, but then seems to almost join the river, giving motorists a close-up view of the rapids, as the water crashes over and among huge boulders. Well worth a stop along this route is the spectacular Grizzly Falls. Allow about an hour. The eastern two-thirds of this road is open during the summer only.

7

Hikes & Other Outdoor Pursuits in Sequoia & Kings Canyon

1 Day Hikes & Scenic Walks

Sequoia & Kings Canyon are an absolute paradise for hikers. This is not only because the parks have a huge network of trails—some 800 miles worth—but because of the vast and relatively untouched wilderness here. In fact, over 85% of these parks—some 736,980 acres—is designated wilderness, accessible only to those on foot or horseback. But it's wrong to assume that this means that these parks are only for the hardcore backpacker. In fact, you can see quite a bit of the parks on a number of short walks and day hikes. In many cases, after just 5 minutes on the trail you'll feel you've left the civilized world behind. At almost any point that you choose to venture away from the highway, you're likely to find an abundance of natural wonders: colorful flora, interesting fauna, and beautiful landscape created over millions of years of solitude. Below, we suggest day hikes that will help you experience the best these parks have to offer. In many cases, an inexpensive trail map will be very helpful; some trail intersections are confusing, and signs can disappear. *Note:* At press time, only Big Trees Trail is wheelchair accessible, but more accessible trails are planned for the Giant Forest area.

NEAR GIANT FOREST

Big Trees Trail   This scenic loop walk among the sequoias skirts a pretty meadow, and has trailside exhibits that explain why this area is such a good habitat for sequoias. There are usually abundant wildflowers in Round Meadow in early summer. The trail is wheelchair accessible, paved with some wooden boardwalk sections.

1.5 miles/1–1½ hr. Easy. Start at the Giant Forest Museum.

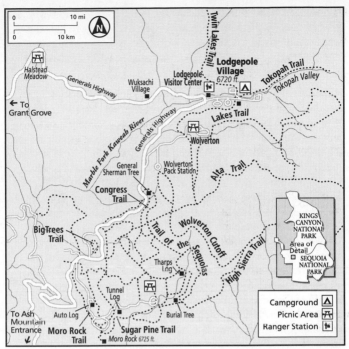

Congress Trail This self-guided walk circles some of Sequoia National Park's most well-known and loved giants. The trail is a paved loop with a 200-foot elevation gain. Here you'll find the General Sherman Tree, considered to be the largest living tree on earth. The Lincoln Tree is nearby, and several clusters of trees include the House and the Senate. Try standing in the middle of these small groups of trees to gain the perspective of an ant at a picnic. The walk is dotted with inviting benches as well.

2 miles/1–3 hr. Easy. Start at the General Sherman Tree, just off the Generals Hwy., 2 miles northeast of Giant Forest Museum.

Crescent Meadow Loop ☙ The meadow is a large, picturesque clearing dotted with high grass and wildflowers, encircled by a forest of firs and sequoias. The park's oldest cabin (Tharp's Log) is along this route as well. This is a particularly nice hike in early morning and at dusk, when the indirect sunlight provides the best pictures.

1.8 miles/1–3 hr. Easy. Begin at the Crescent Meadow parking area.

Hazelwood Nature Trail Follow the signs for a good walk with exhibits that explain the relationship among trees, fire, and humans, while winding among several stands of sequoias.

1 mile/1 hr. Easy. Begin on the south side of the Generals Hwy., across from the rd. to Round Meadow.

High Sierra Trail 🐾🐾 This is one gateway to the backcountry, but the first few miles of the trail also make a great day hike. Along the way you'll find spectacular views of the Kaweah River's middle fork and the Great Western Divide. The trail runs along a south-facing slope, so it's warm in spring and fall. Get an early start in summer. From the trail head, cross two wooden bridges over Crescent Creek until you reach a junction. Tharp's Log is to the left, the High Sierra Trail to the right. Hike uphill through the damage done by the Buckeye Fire of 1988, a blaze ignited by a discarded cigarette 3,000 feet below, near the Kaweah River. After hiking 0.75 miles you'll reach Eagle View, which offers a picturesque vision of the Great Western Divide. On the south side of the canyon are the craggy Castle Rocks. Continue on to see Panther Rock, Alta Peak, and Alta Meadow. At 2.75 miles is a sign for the Wolverton Cutoff, a trail used as a stock route between the Wolverton trail head and the high country. A bit farther on, you'll come upon Panther Creek and a small waterfall. At 3.25 miles is pink-and-gray Panther Rock. Follow a few more creeks to reach the last fork of Panther Creek, running down a steep, eroded ravine.

9 miles/6 hr. Moderate. The trail head is near the restrooms at the Crescent Meadow parking area.

Huckleberry Trail This is a great hike, offering tremendous beauty without the crush of too many people. It passes through forests and meadows, near a 100-year-old cabin, and by an old American Indian village. The first mile of this hike takes you along the Hazelwood Nature Trail (see above). Head south at each junction until you see a big sign with blue lettering that marks the start of the Huckleberry Trail. You'll pass a small creek and meadow before reaching a second sign to Huckleberry Meadow. The next mile is steep and crosses beneath sequoias, dogwoods, and white firs. At the 1.5-mile point is Squatter's Cabin, a log building built in the 1880s. East of the cabin is a trail junction. Head north (left) up a short hill. At the next junction, veer left along the edges of Circle Meadow for about a quarter-mile before you reach another junction. On the right is a short detour to Bear's Bathtub, a pair of sequoias hollowed by fire and filled with water. Legend has it that an old mountain guide named Chester Wright once surprised a bear taking a bath here, hence its name. Continue on the trail heading northeast to the Washington Tree, which is almost as big as the General Sherman Tree, and then on to Alta Trail. Turn west (left) to Little Deer Creek. On both sides of the creek are American Indian mortar holes. At the next junction, head north (right) to return to the Generals Highway and the last leg of the Huckleberry Trail to the parking area.

4 miles/2–3 hr. Moderate. Begin at the Hazelwood Nature Trail parking area, 0.3 miles east of Giant Forest Museum on the Generals Hwy.

Moro Rock 🐾🐾 This walk climbs 300 feet up 400 steps that twist along this gigantic boulder perched perilously on a ridge top. Take it slow. The view from the top is breathtaking, stretching to the Great Western Divide, which looks barren and dark, like the end of the world. Mountains are often snowcapped well into summer. During a full moon, the view is even stranger and more beautiful.

0.25 miles/30 min.–1 hr. Moderate. Begin at the Moro Rock parking area.

Moro Rock and Soldiers Loop Trail This hike cuts cross-country from the Giant Forest Village to Moro Rock. The hike heads through a forest dotted with Giant Sequoias. Be advised that a carpet of ferns occasionally hides the trail. It pops out at Moro Rock, and then it's just a quick heart-thumper to the top (see the trail description above).

4.6 miles/3–4 hr. Moderate. The trail head is just west of Giant Forest Museum.

Trail of the Sequoias This trail offers a longer, more remote hike into Giant Forest, away from the crowds and along some of the more scenic points of the plateau. The first quarter mile is along the Congress Trail before heading uphill at Alta Trail. Look for signs that read TRAIL OF THE SEQUOIAS. After 1.5 miles, including a half-mile steep climb among giant sequoias, you'll encounter the ridge of the Giant Forest. Here you'll find a variety of trees, young and old, fallen and sturdy. Notice the shallow root system of fallen trees and the lightning-blasted tops of others still standing. The trail continues to Log Meadow, past Crescent Meadow, and to Chimney Tree, a sequoia hollowed by fire. At the junction with Huckleberry Trail, follow the blue and green signs straight (north) toward Sherman Tree and back to Congress Trail.

6 miles/4 hr. Moderate. The trail head is at the northeast end of the General Sherman Tree parking area.

NEAR GRANT GROVE

Azalea Trail   This is a pleasant trail at any time, and particularly beautiful in late June and early July when the azaleas along Sequoia Creek are in full fragrant bloom. From the visitor center, walk past the amphitheater to the Sunset Campground and cross CA 180. The first mile joins the South Boundary Trail as it meanders through Wilsonia and crisscrosses Sequoia Creek in a gentle climb. After 1.5 miles, you'll find the third crossing of Sequoia Creek, which may be dry in late summer but the banks are lush with ferns and brightly colored azaleas. Return the way you came.

3 miles/1–2 hr. Easy. The trail head begins at the Kings Canyon Visitor Center.

Big Stump Trail   This trail meanders through what was once a grove of giant sequoias. All that's left today are the old stumps and piles of 100-year-old sawdust. A brochure available at visitor centers describes the logging that occurred here in the 1880s. To continue onward, see the Hitchcock Meadow Trail described below, which leads to Viola Fall.

1 mile/1 hr. Easy. Begin at the Big Stump Picnic Area near the CA 180 entrance to Grant Grove from Kings Canyon.

Dead Giant Loop   This easy, meandering loop trail takes you along a lush meadow to the shell of what was once an impressive forest giant. The Dead Giant Loop and the North Grove Loop (described below) share the first three-quarters of a mile. The trail descends a fire road and after a quarter-mile hits a junction. Take the lower trail, continuing along the fire road. After another half-mile, you'll break off from the North Grove Loop and head south around a lush meadow. It's another quarter-mile to a sign that reads DEAD GIANT. Turn right (west) to see what's left of this large sequoia. The trail climbs slightly as it circles a knoll and comes to Sequoia Lake Overlook. The lake was formed in 1899 when the Kings River Lumber Company built a dam on Mill Flat Creek. The water was diverted down a flume to the town of Sanger. During logging times, millions of board feet of giant sequoias were floated down that flume to be finished at a mill in Sanger. Continue around the loop back to the DEAD GIANT sign and then head back to the parking area.

2.25 miles/1½ hr. Easy. The trail head is at the lower end of the General Grant Tree parking area. It begins near a locked gate with a sign that reads NORTH GROVE LOOP.

General Grant Tree Trail *(Kids*   This walk leads to the huge General Grant Tree, which is the nation's only living national shrine. In 1956, U.S. President Eisenhower gave the Grant Tree this designation

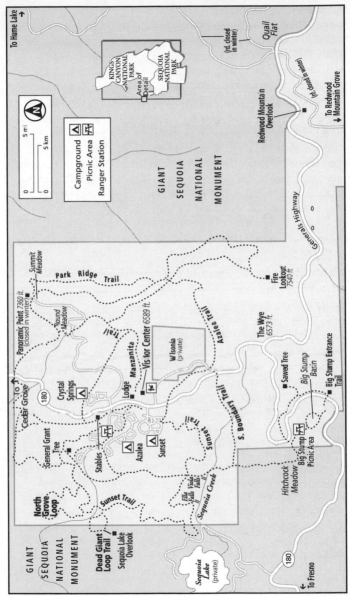

in memory of Americans who gave their lives in wartime. The walk includes signs to help visitors interpret forest features.

0.6 miles/30 min. Easy. Begin at the Grant Tree parking area 1 mile northwest of the visitor center.

Hitchcock Meadow Trail This trail leads to the pretty Viola Fall. The first half-mile mirrors the Big Stump Trail described above. From there, hike another quarter-mile to the Hitchcock sequoia stumps. Notice the small sequoias in this area; they are descendants of the giant sequoias logged in the last century. From here the trail climbs slightly to a ridge, where it re-enters Kings Canyon National Park before descending steeply to Sequoia Creek. Cross the creek on a culvert bridge toward a sign directing hikers to Viola Fall, a series of short steps that, during high water, merge into a single fall. It is dangerous to venture down into the canyon, but above it are several flat places that make great picnic spots.

3.5 miles/2 hr. Easy. Begin at the Big Stump Picnic Area near the entrance to Grant Grove from Kings Canyon.

North Grove Loop This trail follows an abandoned mill road from yesteryear. It cuts through stands of dogwood, sugar pine, sequoia, and white fir. You'll find a large dead sequoia that shows evidence of a fire.

1.2 miles/1–2 hr. Easy. Begin at the lower end of the General Grant Tree parking area.

Park Ridge Trail Begin by walking south along the ridge, where views of the valley and peaks dominate. On a clear day you can see Hume Lake in Sequoia National Forest, the San Joaquin Valley, and occasionally the Coast Range 100 miles away. Return the way you came.

4.7 miles/3 hr. Easy. Begin at the Panoramic Point parking area, a 2.5-mile drive down a steep road from Grant Grove Village.

Sunset Trail This hike climbs 1,400 feet past two waterfalls and a lake. After crossing the highway, the trail moves left around a campground. After 1.25 miles, follow the South Boundary Trail toward Viola Fall. You'll reach a paved road where you can head to the right to see the park's original entrance. Return the way you came, or follow the road to the General Grant Tree parking area and walk to the visitor center.

6 miles/3–4 hr. Moderate to strenuous. Begin across the road from the Kings Canyon Visitor Center.

Impressions

We are gathered here around a tree that is worthy of representing the spirit of America on Christmas Day. That spirit is best expressed in the plain things of life, the love of the family circle, the simple life of the out-of-doors. The tree is a pillar that is a testimony that things of the spirit transcend those of the flesh.

—Colonel John White, former Sequoia & Kings Canyon National Parks superintendent, at a National Christmas Tree ceremony

NEAR CEDAR GROVE

Bubbs Creek Trail   The trail begins by crossing and re-crossing Copper Creek. This site was once an American Indian village, and shards of obsidian can still be found on the ground. After the first mile you'll enter a swampy area that offers a good place to watch for wildlife. The trail here closes in on the river, where deer and bears drink. At 2 miles, you'll come to a junction. The trail to Paradise Valley heads north (left), and the hike to Bubbs Creek veers right and crosses Bailey Bridge, over the South Fork of the Kings River. Continue hiking east over the four small wooden bridges that cross Bubbs Creek. The creek was named after John Bubbs, a prospector and rancher who arrived here in 1864. The trail will climb on the creek's north side, throwing in a few steep switchbacks to keep you alert. The switchbacks provide nice alternating views of the canyon of Paradise Valley and Cedar Grove. At 3 miles is a large emerald pool with waterfalls. Far above is a rock formation known as the Sphinx—John Muir named the feature after Egypt's famous likeness. At 4 miles you enter Sphinx Creek, a nice place to spend the day or night (with a wilderness permit). There are several campsites nearby. Hike back the way you came or along the Sentinel Trail described below.

8 miles/5 hr. Moderate to strenuous. The trail head is at the east end of the parking area at Road's End.

Mist Falls 😊😊   This is one of the more popular trails leading to the backcountry, but it's also a nice day hike. The first 2 miles are dry, until you reach Bubbs Creek Bridge. Take the fork to the left and head uphill. The first waterfall is a pretty spot to take a break. From here, the trail meanders along the river, and through forest and swamp areas, before it comes out at the base of Mist Falls, a wide expanse of a waterfall that flows generously in spring. There are dozens of great picnic spots here and along the way up. Return along the same route, or, at Bubbs Creek Bridge, cross over and head back on the Sentinel Trail described below. Taking Sentinel Trail adds a mile to the hike. From Mist Falls, you can also continue on to Paradise Valley, described below.

8 miles/2–3 hr. Moderate to strenuous. Begin at the short-term parking area at Road's End past Cedar Grove Village and follow the signs.

Muir's Rock Okay, so you can't walk too far, don't have time, and so on. Well, now there's no excuse. This level, simple, short stroll takes you to one of the most historically significant spots in the park's modern-day history. From this wide, flat rock, John Muir used to deliver impassioned speeches about the Sierra. When referring to logging the giant trees, he said that mankind may as well "sell the rain clouds and the snow and the rivers to be cut up and carried away, if that were possible."

100 yd./10 min. Easy. The pulpit is 100 yd. from the parking area at Road's End, along the trail to Zumwalt Meadow.

Paradise Valley 𝒢𝒢 This is a great overnight hike because the valley is so pretty and there's much to explore, but it can also be accomplished as an ambitious day hike. Follow the Mist Falls trail to the falls and then head up 3 miles of switchbacks to Paradise Valley. The valley is 3 miles long, relatively flat, and beautiful. Hike through the valley to connect with the John Muir Trail and the rest of the backcountry, or return the way you came.

12 miles/7–10 hr. Moderate to strenuous. Begin at the short-term parking area at Road's End past Cedar Grove Village and follow the signs.

River Trail This trail heads upstream as it hugs the river and can be shortened if you just want to walk to the waterfalls (.5-mile round-trip) or Zumwalt Meadow (3 miles round-trip; a shorter version is listed below). The waterfalls are 0.25 miles along the trail. The falls are short but powerful—do *not* attempt to climb them. Just north of the falls, back toward the parking area, is a sign that reads ZUMWALT MEADOW—ROAD'S END. Take this trail, which initially hugs the highway before breaking off into a beautiful canyon. At 1.5 miles is the Zumwalt Bridge. If you crossed the bridge, you'd be 0.25 miles from the Zumwalt Meadow parking area. Do not cross the bridge; instead continue onward up the canyon for another 0.25 miles to Zumwalt Meadow. From here there's a slight incline. In 0.5 miles you'll reach a fork; keep right. The rest of the hike follows the riverbank, which sports plenty of swimming and fishing holes. After 2.5 miles you'll come to another footbridge. Cross over and it's a short 0.5 mile walk back to the Road's End parking area, where you can try to catch a ride. Otherwise, retrace your steps back to your car.

5.5 miles/4 hr. Easy. From the Cedar Grove Ranger Station, drive 3.1 miles to the Roaring River Falls parking area.

Sentinel Trail   Essentially, this hike encircles a small length of the south fork of the Kings River. After hiking 2 miles on the river's north side, the trail splits and heads north to Mist Falls and Paradise Valley, or east across Bailey Bridge toward Bubbs Creek. Follow the eastern trail, but instead of going on to Bubbs Creek, follow a sign that reads ROAD'S END—2.6 MILES. It takes you through dense groves of pine and cedar, with occasional views of Grand Sentinel. The trail crosses Avalanche Creek before emerging into a huge meadow and returning to the riverbank. At 2 miles, you can see Muir's Pulpit, the huge boulder described above. At 2.25 miles, you'll find a footbridge that points back to the parking area.

4.6 miles/2–3 hr. Easy. The trail head mirrors the hikes to Bubbs Creek, Mist Falls, and Paradise Valley, described above.

Zumwalt Meadow   This hike takes you across a lovely meadow, with lots of broad views. Cross the bridge and walk left for 100 yards to a fork. Take the trail that leads right for a bird's-eye view of the meadow below before descending 50 feet. The trail runs along the meadow's edge, where the fragrance of ponderosa pine, sugar pine, and incense cedar fill the air. The loop returns along the banks of the South Fork of the Kings River; watch for Grand Sentinel and North Dome rising in the background.

1.5 miles/1 hr. Easy. The trail begins at the Zumwalt Meadow parking area, 1 mile west of Road's End, past Cedar Grove Village.

HIKES ELSEWHERE
Cold Springs Nature Trail (in Mineral King in Sequoia)   This easy loop showcases the natural history and beauty of the region. It passes near private cabins left over from the days before 1978, when the area was added to Sequoia National Park. The walk offers views of the Mineral King Valley and surrounding peaks. It can get hot and dry in summer, so carry additional water.

2 miles/1 hr. Easy. Begin at Mineral King's Cold Springs Campground, across from the ranger station.

Kings River National Recreation Trail   So it's a long drive, but after a hike in upper Kings Canyon, this is a great place to see what the canyon looks like from the bottom. The views here rival anything in the park, with peaks towering overhead and the river rushing nearby. The first mile alternates between rapids and pools that offer great fishing. At 1.5 miles you can see up Converse Creek and its rugged canyon. At 3 miles you'll find Spring Creek, a short but pretty waterfall and a good place to rest. You can turn around here for a total hike of 6 miles, or proceed for the 10-mile option. From this point the trail ascends the steep Garlic Spur, a ridge that ends suddenly at the ledge of the canyon. The trail above Spring Creek is flecked with obsidian, the nearest source of which is the Mono Craters, more than 100 miles to the north. For that reason, many believe this trail was used for trading by the Monache Indians. After the long, steep ascent, the trail heads down to Garlic Meadow Creek. A short distance upstream are large pools and wide resting areas. Beyond the creek, the trail is not maintained.

6–10 miles/4–8 hr., depending on distance traveled. Easy to Spring Creek; strenuous to Garlic Meadow Creek. On CA 180, 6 miles west of Big Stump Entrance, turn north on FS Rd. 12S01, a dirt road marked MCKENZIE HELIPORT, DELILAH LOOKOUT, CAMP 4.5 MILES. Drive 17.5 miles to the Kings River. Turn west and drive another 2.5 miles to Rodgers Crossing. Cross the bridge and turn east, following signs to the Kings River Trail. The trail head is at the east end of a parking lot another 7 miles ahead, at the rd.'s end.

Marble Fork Trail (in Foothills of Sequoia)   This is one of the most scenic hikes in the foothills area. The walk leads to a deep gorge where the roaring Marble Falls spills in a cascade over multi-colored boulders. From the parking area, begin hiking north up the Southern California Edison flume. After crossing the flume on a wooden bridge, watch on the right for a sign to the trail and head east uphill. The trail has some steep switchbacks and is near some large poison oak bushes that sport stems 3 inches wide. Watch out for these bare sticks in late fall and winter. The trail will begin to flatten out and settle into a slight slope for the rest of the hike up to the waterfalls. Look for large yuccas and California bay trees along the way. After 2 miles, you'll be able to see the waterfalls as the hike cuts through white-and-gray marble. Once you reach the falls, it's almost impossible to hike any farther, so don't attempt it. The marble slabs break easily, and boulders in the area can get slick. Be extra careful when the water is high. This is a good hike year-round but can be hot during summer. Upon your return, be sure to check yourself thoroughly for ticks.

6 miles/4–6 hr. Strenuous. Follow the dirt rd. at the upper end of Potwisha Campground, which is 3.8 miles east of the Ash Mountain Entrance. There is a small parking area past campsite no. 16.

Potwisha and River's Edge   This was the site of an American Indian village known as Potwisha, home to a tribe of Monache. The main village was just about where the dump station is now. On the bedrock are mortar holes where the women ground acorns into meal. From here the trail continues up the river to a sandy beach and a good swimming hole. The trail turns east upstream before the suspension bridge, then northward up a short but steep hill to the road. Turn west (left) and hike the short distance back to the parking area.

0.5 miles/30 min. Easy. From the Ash Mountain Entrance, take the highway to the Potwisha Campground. At the campground entrance (which will be to your left), turn right down a paved rd. toward an RV dump station until it hits a dead end at a parking area. Continue toward the river on a footpath to open bedrock.

Wildman Meadow (National Forest)   This hike through the Monarch Wilderness starts with a relatively easy trek to Deer Cove. After reaching Deer Cove, it's a steep ascent to 7,500 feet—a 1,900-foot gain in 5 miles. From Deer Cove, hike 3.5 miles to a sandy knoll, where there is a good view into the rugged canyon drainage area of Grizzly Creek. At 6.5 miles, you'll top the ridge and cross over to the north-facing slope. A quick drop lands you in Wildman Meadow.

14 miles/10 hr. Strenuous. Deer Cove Trailhead is just north of Calif. 180, 2.5 miles west of Cedar Grove and the Kings Canyon border in the Sequoia National Forest. See the trail head directions for Deer Cove Trail, above.

2 Other Sports & Activities

CROSS-COUNTRY SKIING   There are 35 miles of marked backcountry trails in the parks. Call ✆ 559/335-5500 for information in Grant Grove and ✆ 559/565-4070 for information in the Giant Forest area.

FISHING   Open all year for trout fishing—rainbow, brook, German brown, and golden trout—are the **Kaweah** drainage, the parks' lakes, and a section of the south fork of the **Kings River.** Most other waters are open for trout fishing from late April to mid-November, and for other species year-round. California fishing licenses (available at stores in the park) are required for anglers 16 and older, and you should also get a copy of the National Park Service's fishing regulations, available at visitor centers.

HORSEBACK RIDING   Guided horseback and mule rides and overnight pack trips are offered by concessionaires in both parks and the adjacent national monument during the summer. In Kings Canyon, **Cedar Grove Pack Station** (✆ 559/565-3464 summer, 559/337-2314 winter) is located about 1 mile east of Cedar Grove

Village; and **Grant Grove Stables** (✆ **559/335-9292** summer, 559/ 337-2314 winter) is located near Grant Grove Village. In Giant Sequoia National Monument, **Horse Corral Pack Station** is located on Big Meadows Road, 10 miles east of Generals Highway (✆ **559/565-3404** summer, 559/564-6429 winter; www.horsecorral packers.com). The pack stations offer hourly rides as well as overnight treks, while the stables offer day rides only. Rates range from $25 to $30 for a 1-hour ride to $75 to $100 for a full day in the saddle; call for current charges for pack trips.

SNOWSHOEING   On winter weekends, rangers lead introductory snowshoe hikes in **Grant Grove** (✆ **559/565-4307**) and **Giant Forest** (✆ **559/565-4436**). Snowshoes are provided, but a $1 donation is requested.

WHITE-WATER BOATING   The **Kaweah** and **Upper Kings rivers** in the parks are not open to boating (neither kayaks nor inflatable rafts), but several companies run trips just outside the parks. You're guaranteed to get wet, but this roller-coaster ride through the rapids is thrilling, and a great way to not only see, but also experience, these scenic rivers. **Kaweah White Water Adventures** (✆ **800/229-8658** or 559/561-1000; www.kaweahwhite water.com) runs class III, IV, and V trips (rated moderate to difficult) on the Kaweah River. Trips are run in inflatable kayaks or rafts and are offered from spring to early fall. Prices range from about $40 per person for a 2-hour trip to $130 per person (including lunch) for a full day. Offering trips on the Kaweah, Kings, Kern, and Merced rivers is **Whitewater Voyages** (✆ **800/400-RAFT;** www.whitewatervoyages.com), with rates that range from $109 to $209 (including lunch) for full-day trips, and multiday trips are also available (call for rates). **Kings River Expeditions** (✆ **800/846-3674** or 559/233-4881; www.kingsriver.com) specializes in rafting trips on the Kings. For 1-day trips they charge $99 to $130 in spring, and $130 to $175 from mid-May until the season ends. Overnight trips are also available (call for rates).

3 Exploring the Backcountry

Finding quiet and solitude is not nearly as difficult here as it is in Yosemite. Mineral King and the Giant Forest in Sequoia, and Cedar Grove in Kings Canyon, are the main points of entry into the backcountry, but the wilderness here is never farther away than 5 miles in any direction. It surrounds the park, and just about any hike that lasts more than an hour will get you into the wild. The park is crisscrossed by numerous trails leading into the high country, including the world-famous Pacific Crest Trail, as well as the John Muir Trail, which begins in Yosemite and ends at Sequoia's Mount Whitney.

Mineral King is a quiet spot that attracts few people to its 11 trails because the road to the glacial valley is so difficult to drive. Avalanches have swept swathes of trees aside and the valley floor is covered with wild meadows. Higher up, there are woods of red fir, white fir, and lodgepole pine. The landscape is rocky but colorful. Alpine trails begin at 7,500 feet and climb from there.

Cedar Grove in Kings Canyon is at the dead end of CA 180. From here, to the north and east, the park is inaccessible to vehicular traffic. Hikes from here head out toward the Rae Lakes Loop, Monarch Wilderness, and beyond.

PREPARING FOR YOUR TRIP TO THE BACKCOUNTRY

Be sure to get a detailed topographical map before setting off on any overnight hike. Maps are available at all ranger stations and at visitor centers throughout the park. In addition to this book, you may want to pick up a copy of "Backcountry Basics," a free trip-planning guide for the wilderness areas of the parks, which can be obtained at park visitor centers, or call ℂ **559/565-3341** to request one.

PERMITS & FEES All overnight backpacking trips require a wilderness permit, available by mail, by fax, or in person at the ranger station closest to the hike you want to take. First-come, first-served permits can be issued the morning of your trip or after 1pm on the preceding afternoon. In summer, permits cost $20 for the first two campers and more for additional people; in winter, they're free.

Reservations can be made 21 or more days in advance, starting March 1. To reserve a permit, you must provide a name, address, telephone number, the number of people in your party, the method of travel (snowshoe, horse, foot), number of stock if applicable, start and end dates, start and end trail heads, a principal destination, and a rough itinerary. Mail the application to **Wilderness Permit Reservations,** Sequoia & Kings Canyon National Parks, Three Rivers, CA 93271, or fax it to **559/565-4239.** Reserved permits must be picked up by 9am. If you're delayed, call the ranger station or you risk forfeiting your permit. If your hike crosses agency boundaries, get the permit from the agency on whose land the hike begins. Only one permit is required.

For hikes beginning in the Sequoia National Forest (or in Giant Sequoia National Monument, which is managed as a section of this national forest), pick up your permits at the ranger district offices in

Blackrock, Lake Isabella, Kernville, Springville, or Dunlap, or contact **Sequoia National Forest,** 900 W. Grand Ave., Porterville, CA 93257 (© **559/784-1500;** www.fs.fed.us/r5/sequoia). The national forest wraps around the southern and western portions of Sequoia & Kings Canyon National Parks. Permits are free and there are no quotas on trails in this forest.

In Sierra National Forest, permits are also free, but reservations are $5 and quotas apply from the last Friday in June to September 15. Permits are issued at the ranger station closest to your trail head. This forest lies west and north of Kings Canyon National Park. For maps and further information, contact **Sierra National Forest** at 1600 Tollhouse Rd., Clovis, CA 93611 (© **559/297-0706;** www.fs. fed.us/r5/sierra).

The Inyo National Forest administers areas that stretch from the Sierra Crest to Owens Valley. Most trails here have quotas, and free permits are required. Reservations are available 3 months in advance and cost $5 per person; $15 for Mount Whitney, which are issued through a lottery. For reservations, contact **Wilderness Permit Reservations,** Inyo National Forest, 351 Pacu Lane, Suite 200, Bishop, CA 93514 (© **760/873-2483** 10am–4pm Mon–Fri, daily in summer; fax 760/873-2484; information only 760/873-2485; www.fs.fed.us/r5/inyo).

Food drops can be arranged in advance, but are difficult without the help of an outfitter. No packaging from the drop may be left behind. Call the parks' wilderness office (© **559/565-3708,** then follow the instructions) for information. Food can also be mailed to the Cedar Grove and Mineral King ranger stations. Packages are held for 3 weeks from the date received or 3 weeks after the expected pickup date, whichever is longer. Use regular U.S. Mail. Address packages with your name, identification as a trail hiker, and pickup date, all on the first line. Address packages in care of the Cedar Grove Ranger Station, Box 926, Kings Canyon National Park, CA 93633, or in care of the Mineral King Ranger Station, Star Route, Three Rivers, CA 93271.

The Cedar Grove Ranger Station is usually open daily from 8am to 5pm between Memorial Day and Labor Day. The Mineral King Ranger Station is open from 8am to 4pm from Memorial Day weekend to early October.

SPECIAL WARNINGS Be aware of bears that frequent these regions. In the summer months, mosquitoes and sunburn are real problems. Stay off high peaks during thunderstorms and don't attempt any climb if it looks as though a storm is rolling in; exposed peaks are often struck by lightning. And finally, many of these routes are buried under snow in winter. For information on what to bring on your overnight hike, refer to "Backpacking for Beginners" in chapter 4.

Note: There are 14 ranger stations in the wilderness of the park. Eight are along the John Muir and Pacific Crest trails. Another six are in the southern part of the park in the Sequoia backcountry. Most are not staffed fall through spring. To find out which ranger station is closest to your trail head, consult the park map handed out free at all entrances.

OVERNIGHT HIKES

High Sierra Trail   This trail is a popular route into the backcountry. Some use it as a one-way passage to Mount Whitney. The trail gets a lot of sun, so begin early in the day. From the parking area, head out on a paved trail to the south (straight), over several bridges, and to a junction. Turn right onto the High Sierra Trail. You will pass Eagle View, the Wolverton Cutoff, and Panther Creek. Hike at least 3 miles before setting up camp.

10 miles/5 hr. Take CA 198 to Giant Forest and proceed to Crescent Meadow Rd. Bear right at the junction, passing the signed parking area for Moro Rock. The rd. ends at the Crescent Meadow parking area.

Jennie Lakes Trail   This is a nice overnight hike that's not too demanding and can be further extended into the Jennie Lakes Wilderness Area. From the parking area, cross through the campground and move across Big Meadow Creek. From here the trail climbs. At Fox Meadow, there is a wooden trail sign and a register for hikers to sign. At the next junction, head right toward Jennie Lake (left goes toward the Weaver Lake Trail) and up to Poop Out Pass. From here it's a drop down to the Boulder Creek drainage area and on to emerald-green Jennie Lake. This hike can be combined with a second day hike to Weaver Lake. Just retrace your steps to the Weaver Lake turnoff. Weaver Lake is a relatively warm mountain lake surrounded by blueberry bushes that reportedly weigh heavy with fresh fruit in July. Camp at least one quarter-mile from the lakeshore.

12 miles/7 hr. Moderate to strenuous. From Grant Grove, drive about 7 miles south on the Generals Hwy. to the turnoff for Big Meadows Campground. The trail head and parking are on the south side of the rd. next to a ranger's station.

Lakes Trail   This trail moves along a string of tarns—high mountain lakes created by the scouring action of glaciers thousands of years ago. Heather Lake and Pear Lake are popular destinations along this route. From the trail head, go straight ahead (east), avoiding the Long Meadow Trail. Climb up a moraine ridge and soon you'll be hiking above Wolverton Creek, which darts through small meadows strewn with wildflowers. At a junction with the Panther Gap Trail, head left toward Heather Lake. At a second junction you'll have to choose your direction. To the right is Hump Trail, a steep but always open trail, with no extreme drop-offs. To the left is the Watchtower Trail, which moves along a granite ledge blasted in the rock with dynamite. With the Tokopah Valley far below, the Watchtower Trail hike is not for those who suffer vertigo. Both trails wind up at Heather Lake. Camping is not allowed here but is okay farther up the trail at Pear and Emerald lakes.

12.5 miles/7 hr. Moderate to strenuous. From Giant Forest, drive north on the Generals Hwy. to the Wolverton parking area. The trail head is on the left of the parking lot as you enter from the hwy.

8

Where to Stay & Eat in Sequoia & Kings Canyon

With campgrounds scattered throughout these parks and the nearby Giant Sequoia National Monument, you should have little trouble finding a spot to pitch your tent or park your RV. However, be aware that no RV hookups are available in the parks or monument, and full-service commercial RV parks in the surrounding towns are in short supply. Those who prefer "roughing it" in comfortable hotels will find a variety of options, both within and outside the parks, ranging from inexpensive mom-and-pop–style motels to historic bed-and-breakfast inns and delightful mountain lodges. As for food, there are quite a few choices, so you should have no worries about going hungry.

The three primary gateway communities discussed in this chapter are all along CA 198. Visalia, which is 36 miles from the park boundary at the Ash Mountain Entrance, is the largest town in the area, with the most facilities. Closer to the parks are tiny Lemon Cove, 11 miles from the park boundary, and Three Rivers, 7 miles from the park boundary. From several miles inside the Ash Mountain Entrance to Giant Forest, the Generals Highway is narrow and winding and not recommended for vehicles more than 22 feet long; these should enter the parks from CA 180.

1 Lodging

INSIDE THE PARKS

Lodging inside these national parks ranges from rustic cabins to pleasant and well-equipped motel-style lodging, usually with a mountain-lodge atmosphere and great views. There are also several good lodging choices in the nearby Giant Sequoia National Monument and in the gateway towns of Visalia, Three Rivers, and Lemon Cove (see "Lodging Outside the Parks," below).

Cedar Grove Lodge ℛ This motel offers comfortable rooms on the bank of the Kings River. Getting here is half the fun—it's a 36-mile drive down a winding highway that provides beautiful vistas along the way. The rooms here are standard motel accommodations—clean and comfortable, but nothing special. What you're really paying for is the location, surrounded by tall trees with a pretty river running by. Most of the rooms are above the Cedar Grove Café (see "Where to Eat," later in this chapter) and boast communal decks with river views. However, we prefer the three smaller and not-quite-as-attractively-appointed rooms on ground level, with private patios looking right out on the river. A 24-hour pay phone is available.

CA 180, Cedar Grove, Kings Canyon National Park (mail: Sequoia–Kings Canyon Park Services Company, 5755 E. Kings Canyon Rd., Ste. 101, Fresno, CA 93727). 🕿 **866/ 522-6966** or 559/452-1081. Fax 559/452-1353. www.sequoia-kingscanyon.com. 18 units. $109–$125 double. AE, DISC, MC, V. Closed Nov–Apr. *In room:* A/C, no phone; ground-floor rooms: fridge, microwave.

Grant Grove Cabins *(Value)*   Although these are all cabins, there's a wide range of amenities and prices to be found here, from hand-somely restored cabins with private bathrooms that ooze historic ambience, to rustic tent-cabins that simply provide a comfortable bed out of the weather at a very low price. Those who want to "rough it" in style should reserve one of the nine cabins, built in the 1920s, that have electricity, indoor plumbing, and full private bath-rooms. A bit less modern, but still quite comfortable, are the 43 rus-tic cabins that have kerosene lanterns for light and a shared bathhouse. Some are rustic wooden cabins; others, available in sum-mer only, have wood floors and walls but canvas roofs. All cabins have full linen service. It's a 10-minute walk from the cabins to the Grant Grove visitor center, and the Grant Grove Restaurant is also nearby (see "Where to Eat," later in this chapter).

CA 180, Grant Grove Village, Kings Canyon National Park (mail: Sequoia–Kings Canyon Park Services Company, 5755 E. Kings Canyon Rd., Ste. 101, Fresno, CA 93727). 🕿 **866/522-6966** or 559/452-1081. Fax 559/452-1353. www.sequoia-kings canyon.com. 53 units (9 with private bathroom). $57–$79 cabin with shared bathroom, $115–$125 cabins with private bathroom. Register at Grant Grove Village Registration Center, between the restaurant and gift shop. AE, DISC, MC, V. *In room:* No phone.

John Muir Lodge *(R)*   This handsome log lodge, built in 1998, looks perfect in its beautiful national-park setting. It's an excellent choice for visitors who want quiet, comfortable, modern rooms, with full bathrooms and coffeemakers, located in a forest environ-ment. Standard rooms offer two queen beds and wonderful views of the surrounding forest. A mountain-lodge atmosphere prevails. Suites consist of two connecting standard rooms, except that one of the rooms has a queen bed and a queen sofa sleeper instead of two queens.

CA 180, Grant Grove Village, Kings Canyon National Park (mail: Sequoia–Kings Canyon Park Services Company, 5755 E. Kings Canyon Rd., Ste. 101, Fresno, CA 93727). ℭ **866/ 522-6966** or 559/452-1081. Fax 559/452-1353. www.sequoia-kingscanyon.com. 30 units, including 6 suites. $159 rooms; $259 suites. Register at Grant Grove Village Registration Center, between the restaurant and gift shop. AE, DISC, MC, V.

Silver City Mountain Resort 🏂 *Finds*   An excellent choice for those seeking a woodsy experience in a handsome cabin surrounded by forest. There are three types of cabins here, with a variety of bed combinations (some cabins sleep up to eight) and woodstoves for heat. (Wood is provided.) Blankets and pillows are provided, but guests need to bring their own sheets, pillowcases, bath and kitchen towels, paper towels, and tall trash bags for all cabins. The top-of-the-line Swiss Chalets are finished in knotty pine with completely equipped kitchens, full bathrooms, Internet access, and an outdoor barbecue. The mid-level units, dubbed "Comfy Cabins," are two-bedroom units with complete kitchens, propane wall lamps and kerosene lanterns, small restrooms with toilets but no showers (there is a centrally located bathhouse), and decks with barbecue grills. "Rustic Cabins," which were built in the 1930s, are the most basic units, with light from kerosene and propane lamps, a camp kitchen with a gas stove and an oven, a cold-water sink, and an outdoor deck with barbecue. Some "Rustic Cabins" have refrigerators, and all share the showers and toilets in the central bathhouse. There is also one small one-room cabin, with a double bed and little else, that sleeps two. Cabins get booked early, with reservations accepted in January for the entire year. There is a 2- to 3-night minimum for the Swiss Chalets and Comfy Cabins. All units are nonsmoking.

Mineral King, Sequoia National Park (mail: 2570 Rodman Dr., Los Osos, CA 93402). ℭ **559/561-3223,** or 805/528-2730 in winter. Fax 805/528-8039. www.silvercity resort.com. 14 cabins, 7 with shared central bathhouse. $75–$295 double. Discounts approximately June 1–15 and after Sept 18. MC, V. Closed Nov–May. Take CA 198 through Three Rivers to the Mineral King turnoff. Silver City is a little more than halfway between Lookout Point and Mineral King. **Amenities:** Restaurant; bakery; breakfast bar; store.

Wuksachi Lodge 🏂   Built in 1999, the Wuksachi Village and Lodge is the newest development in the park. Guest rooms are located in three buildings separated from the lodge by parking lots. The best views are out the windows, where the forest and surrounding mountains dominate the scene. The standard rooms have one king or two queen beds and a small desk; deluxe rooms are larger, with two queen beds or a king and a sofa bed, plus a table and two chairs; and what are called superior rooms are minisuites, with two queen beds or one king, plus a sofa bed in an alcove sitting area with a sliding door (a good place for your teenager!). All the rooms are a healthy walk from the parking lots (especially when loaded down with luggage), but bellmen in golf carts are available.

CA 180 and 198 (P.O. Box 89), Sequoia National Park, CA 93262. ⓒ 888/252-5757 or 559/253-2199. www.visitsequoia.com. 102 units. May–Oct and holidays $155–$230; Nov–Apr (except holidays) $99–$149. AE, DISC, MC, V. **Amenities:** Dining room (see "Where to Eat," later in this chapter); lounge. *In room:* TV, dataport, fridge, coffeemaker, hair dryer, ski storage rack.

LODGING OUTSIDE THE PARKS

Additional lodging choices are found outside park boundaries, and in most cases you'll be passing these facilities and a few others as you travel to different sections of the parks.

IN GIANT SEQUOIA NATIONAL MONUMENT

Montecito–Sequoia Lodge ⓖ (Kids)   The Montecito offers comfortable rooms in a well-stocked resort that caters to families with children and large groups, although guests of all ages will enjoy this well-run facility. It's open year-round and offers recreation of all types—from fishing to fencing to cross-country skiing (85 miles of groomed trails begin here). Rooms, which all have private bathrooms, are located in four separate buildings; 13 cabins share two bathhouses. Bed types and number vary, with units that sleep from two to eight. The property has a mountain-lodge atmosphere. Meals are served buffet style. The Lodge has a small lake, with seasonal sailing and canoeing. It also offers snowshoeing and ice skating.

8000 Generals Hwy., Giant Sequoia National Monument (mail: Box 858, 8000 Generals Hwy., Kings Canyon National Park, CA 93633). ⓒ 800/227-9900, 800/843-8667, or 559/565-3388. Fax 559/565-3223. www.mslodge.com. 36 units, plus 13 cabins that share 2 bathhouses. $55–$139 per night per person; vacation packages available for about $500 to $1,000 per guest for 4 to 6 days. Rates include breakfast and dinner. AE, DISC, MC, V. Take CA 180 into Kings Canyon National Park, turn right at the fork, and drive 8 miles south to the lodge entrance, turn right, and follow the rd. about ½ mile to the parking lot. **Amenities:** Dining room; bar; large, heated outdoor pool; 2 outdoor tennis courts; Jacuzzi; watersports equipment; children's and teen programs; game room; self-serve laundry.

Stony Creek Lodge   This small, recently renovated lodge offers comfortable, motel-style accommodations in a pretty setting in the new Giant Sequoia National Monument, which is located 20 minutes south of Grant Grove in Sequoia National Forest. Rooms are pleasant and sleep from two to four. The lodge's lobby is inviting, with a massive stone fireplace. There's also a pizzeria and a newly minted gas station here.

Generals Hwy., Giant Sequoia National Monument (mail: Sequoia–Kings Canyon Park Services Company, 5755 E. Kings Canyon Rd., Ste. 101, Fresno, CA 93727). © 866/ 522-6966 or 559/452-1081. Fax 559/452-1353. www.sequoia-kingscanyon.com. 11 units. $135–$145 double. AE, DISC, MC, V. Closed Sept–May. Take the Stony Creek Village exit off the Generals Hwy., between Grant Grove Village and Wuksachi. **Amenities:** Restaurant; self-service laundry; store.

IN THE NEARBY GATEWAY TOWNS

In addition to the properties discussed below, reliable chains in Visalia include the **Best Western Visalia Inn,** 623 W. Main St., Visalia, CA 93291 (© **877/500-4771** or 559/732-4561), which has rates of $79 double; and the **Super 8,** 4801 W. Noble Ave., Visalia, CA 93277 (© **800/800-8000** or 559/627-2885), charging $65 double. Chain options in Three Rivers include the **Best Western Holiday Lodge,** 40105 Sierra Dr. (P.O. Box 129), Three Rivers, CA 93271 (© **888/523-9909** or 559/561-4119), which charges $79 to $139 double; and the **Holiday Inn Express,** 40820 Sierra Dr., Three Rivers, CA 93271 (© **800/465-4329** or 559/561-9000), charging $89 to $119 double.

Ben Maddox House 𝓡𝓡𝓡   Our top choice for an enchanting place to stay in the Visalia area, the Ben Maddox House is named for one of Visalia's most prominent citizens during the late 1800s and early 1900s. Ben Maddox started the local newspaper and the area's first electric company. Located 4 blocks from downtown Visalia on a street with a number of other Victorian homes, the inn is replete with gardens, decks, a small finch aviary, and a citrus orchard that includes a 100-year-old lemon tree that is still producing. Large palm trees grace the front yard. The house itself is impressive, with a large, triangular gable and a long covered porch, where you can relax on the porch swing and watch the world go slowly by.

The house is furnished with antiques, including many Victorian pieces, and the comfortable and attractive guest rooms have 14-foot ceilings and white-oak floors. One room has a California king-size bed; the rest each have one queen bed. Rooms are appropriate for only two people. All rooms are nonsmoking.

601 N. Encina St., Visalia, CA 93291. © **800/401-9800** or 559/739-0721. Fax 559/ 625-0420. www.benmaddoxhouse.com. 6 units. $85–$130 double. Rates include full breakfast. AE, DISC, MC, V. Open Apr–Oct. Appropriate for children 13 and older. **Amenities:** Large outdoor swimming pool; Wi-Fi network. *In room:* Cable TV/VCR, dataport, fridge, hair dryer, iron.

Buckeye Tree Lodge ☜ *Value*   Located just a half-mile from the entrance to Sequoia National Park, this motel offers affordable and attractive rooms, not to mention rolling lawns that end at a picturesque river, and every room has a patio or balcony offering splendid views. Rooms are clean, basic motel units, with a king bed or two queens. Eight rooms have showers only; the rest have shower/tub combos. There is also a separate cottage that sleeps up to five.

46000 Sierra Dr., Three Rivers, CA 93271. ✆ **559/561-5900.** www.buckeyetree.com. 12 units. $58–$130 double; $99–$210 cottage. Rates include continental breakfast. AE, DC, DISC, MC, V. Pets accepted but must be declared when making reservations. **Amenities:** Outdoor heated pool. *In room:* A/C, cable TV/VCR (video rentals available), microwave (in some rooms), fridge, coffeemaker.

Lake Elowin Resort ☜☜   Undoubtedly one of the best places to stay in the Sierra, this 70-year-old resort is what a resort should be—a place to get away from it all. There are no phones and no televisions, just rustic but clean cabins nestled under huge trees, all looking out at Lake Elowin, a small body of water above the Kaweah River. Milton Melkonian purchased the resort in the 1970s with the idea of creating a place to coexist with nature, and he is fastidious about his creation, which now attracts all sorts of creative types, such as writers and artists, as well as anyone seeking an escape. Cabins can accommodate two to six people. We especially like cabin no. 1, which sits close to the lake and has a delightful view from the kitchen window, and Master Cabin, which boasts a fireplace, a deck, and a Jacuzzi. All cabins include linens and towels, pots and pans, kitchen utensils, barbecues, and canoes. You bring the food, sunblock, and a good attitude. The entire property is nonsmoking; guests must actually sign a contract to not smoke here.

43840 Dineley Dr., Three Rivers, CA 93271. ✆ **559/561-3460.** Fax 559/561-1300. www.lake-elowin.com. 10 cabins with showers only. $120–$145 double; $130–$225 cabin; $300 Master Cabin. AE, DISC, MC, V. From eastbound Sierra Dr. in Three Rivers, about 2½ miles before the park entrance, turn left on Dineley Dr. (the street sign says DINLEY) and drive across a bridge. Bear right, and it's less than ½ mile to the resort's driveway. **Amenities:** Swimming hole; massage; free canoe usage. *In room:* A/C, kitchens.

Plantation Bed & Breakfast ☜☜☜   Step into the Old South at this fun bed-and-breakfast, where the inspiration for the room names and decor comes from characters in the novel and film, *Gone With the Wind.* Those seeking a quietly conservative atmosphere will want to request the Ashley Wilkes Room, which has a king bed; while honeymooners might enjoy the luxurious Scarlett O'Hara Room, with a king bed, velvet loveseat, fireplace, and marble bathroom containing a Jacuzzi and separate shower. Our favorite, though, is the Belle Watling Room, done up in an elegant bordello style, with a king-size bed with an enormous mirror next to it, a red crystal chandelier, and a claw-foot bathtub with a (tastefully done) Renaissance-style nude painted on the side. Two rooms have showers only, while the others have showers and tubs.

Secluded in an orange grove, and watched over by an almost life-size statue of a mermaid, are a large swimming pool (19 ft. wide by 38 ft. long by 4½ ft. deep) and an oversized Jacuzzi, which are available at all hours. The wonderful breakfasts include an abundance of fresh fruit, homemade granola, and a hot entree such as mushroom asparagus crepes, croissant French toast, or spinach frittata. All rooms here are nonsmoking.

33038 CA 198, Lemon Cove, CA 93244 (on CA 198, 16 miles west of the park entrance). (℃) **800/240-1466** or 559/597-2555. Fax 559/597-2551. www.plantation bnb.com. 8 units. $139–$299 double. Rates include full breakfast. AE, DC, DISC, MC, V. **Amenities:** Large pool; Jacuzzi. *In room:* Cable TV, VCR (most rooms), no phone.

Sierra Lodge *(Value)* Built to resemble a Swiss chalet, this small motel, about 3 miles from the national park entrance, offers well-maintained rooms and suites in a very scenic setting along a river, among 150-year-old oak trees. The rooms range from quite small to fairly spacious, and have a lot of homey touches such as decorative plates, artificial flowers, and the like. Standard rooms offer a variety of bed options—two doubles, one queen, or one king. The suites are more luxurious. The VIP Suite would be ideal for two couples traveling together. It has two bedrooms (one queen bed in each), a full bathroom, a kitchenette, a living room with a handsome stone fireplace, and a private balcony with splendid views. Some rooms have fireplaces; eight have showers only, the rest have showers and small bathtubs.

43175 Sierra Dr., Three Rivers, CA 93271. (℃) **800/367-8879** or 559/561-3681. Fax 559/561-3264. www.sierra-lodge.com. 17 units, 5 suites. $58–$99 double; $130–$200 suites. Rates about 20% lower in winter. Rates include morning pastries and coffee and tea. AE, DC, DISC, MC, V. **Amenities:** Small outdoor pool; barbecues. *In room:* A/C, TV, kitchenettes, fridge, coffeemaker.

Spalding House This Colonial Revival home—built in 1901 by local lumberman W. R. Spalding—offers suites only, each with a sitting room and private bathroom. (One has a shower/tub combo; the others have showers only.) The owners restored the entire home themselves, decorating it in the style of the early 1900s with Oriental rugs, antiques, and reproductions. Two suites have queen-size beds; the other has a double bed. We especially like the Spalding Suite, which has a four-post, colonial-style, queen-size bed and a delightful sitting room with wicker furniture and lots of windows. Common areas include the library, which contains more than 1,500 books, and the music room, with its 1923 Steinway grand player piano. Breakfast is a major event here: a five-course meal that includes hot entrees such as cheese blintzes, apple crepes, or omelets, and might also include baked grapefruit, sausage or ham, or yogurt dishes. The inn is totally nonsmoking.

631 N. Encina St., Visalia, CA 93291. ℂ 559/739-7877. Fax 559/625-0902. www.thespaldinghouse.com. 3 suites. From $95 double. Rates include full breakfast. AE, MC, V. *In room:* A/C, no phone.

2 Camping

There are numerous camping opportunities both within and surrounding Sequoia & Kings Canyon National Parks. Brief descriptions of individual campgrounds follow, and you'll find additional details in the campground chart in this chapter.

It's important to remember that when camping in this area, proper food storage is *required* for the sake of the black bears in the parks as well as your safety. See local bulletin boards for instructions.

Note: You'll need a wilderness permit to stay overnight in the backcountry, see "Exploring the Backcountry" in chapter 7.

IN SEQUOIA NATIONAL PARK

The only National Park campgrounds that accept reservations are Dorst and Lodgepole (ℂ 800/365-2267; http://reservations.nps.gov), which accept reservations up to 5 months in advance; the other campgrounds are first-come, first-served. Additional information on the National Park campgrounds (but not reservations) can be obtained by calling the general Sequoia & Kings Canyon information line at ℂ 559/565-3341.

The two biggest campgrounds in the park are in the Lodgepole area. The **Lodgepole Campground,** which has flush toilets, is often crowded, but it's pretty and near some spectacular big trees. Nearby backcountry trails offer some solitude. Close to the campground are a grocery store, restaurant, visitor center, children's nature center, evening ranger programs, and gift shop. From Giant Forest Museum, drive 5 miles northeast on the Generals Highway.

Dorst Campground, located 14 miles northwest of Giant Forest via the Generals Highway, is a high-elevation campground that offers easy access to Muir Grove and some pleasant backcountry trails. It has flush toilets and evening ranger programs. Group campsites are also available here by reservation.

In the Foothills area, **Potwisha Campground** is a small campground, with well-spaced sites tucked beneath oak trees along the Marble Fork of the Kaweah River. The campground has flush toilets. However, it does get hot in summer. From the Ash Mountain Entrance, drive 3 miles northeast on the Generals Highway to the campground entrance. The **Buckeye Flat Campground** 🌲, which is open to tents only, is also set among oaks along the Middle Fork of the Kaweah River, and although it also gets hot in summer, it is among our favorites due to its scenic beauty. It has flush toilets. From the Ash Mountain Entrance, drive about 6 miles northeast on the Generals Highway to the Hanging Rock Picnic Area. From there, follow signs to the campground, which is several miles down a narrow, winding road. **South Fork Campground** is the smallest and most remote campground in the park, located just inside Sequoia's southwestern boundary. It is set along the South Fork of the Kaweah River and has pit toilets only. From the town of Three Rivers, go east on South Fork Road 23 miles to the campground.

The two campgrounds in the Mineral King area are open to tents only—no RVs or trailers. **Atwell Mill Campground** is a pretty, small campground near the East Fork of the Kaweah River, at Atwell Creek. It has pit toilets. From Three Rivers, take Mineral King Road east for 20 miles to the campground. **Cold Springs Campground,** which also has pit toilets, is a beautiful place to stay—it's just not very accessible. Once you get there, however, you'll be rewarded with beautiful scenery. It's also a good starting point for many backcountry hikes, as it's near the Mineral King Ranger Station. From Three Rivers, take Mineral King Road east for 25 miles to the campground.

IN KINGS CANYON NATIONAL PARK

All of the campgrounds in Kings Canyon are first-come, first-served only (reservations are not available), and all have flush toilets. Additional information can be obtained by calling the general Sequoia & Kings Canyon information line at © **559/565-3341.**

In the Grant Grove area, there are three attractive campgrounds near the big trees—**Azalea, Crystal Springs,** and **Sunset**—which have a nice woodsy feel, are close to park facilities, and offer evening ranger programs. To get to them from the Big Stump Entrance, take CA 180 east about 1¾ miles.

Several pleasant campgrounds lie in the Cedar Grove Village area, all accessed from CA 180, and all fairly close to the facilities in Cedar Grove Village. **Sentinel,** the first to open for the season, tends to fill up quickly. **Moraine** is the farthest from the crowds. **Sheep**

Sequoia & Kings Canyon Campgrounds

CAMPGROUND	ELEV. (FT.)	TOTAL SITES	RV HOOKUPS	DUMP STATION	TOILETS	DRINKING WATER	SHOWERS	FIRE PITS/ GRILLS	LAUNDRY	PUBLIC PHONES	RESERVATIONS POSSIBLE	FEES	OPEN
INSIDE SEQUOIA NATIONAL PARK													
Atwell Mill	6,650	21	0	No	Yes	Yes	No	Yes	No	No	No	$12	May–Oct
Buckeye Flat	2,800	28	0	No	Yes	Yes	No	Yes	No	No	No	$18	Apr–Oct
Cold Springs	7,500	40	0	No	Yes	Yes	No	Yes	No	Yes	No	$12	May–Oct
Dorst	6,700	204	0	Yes	Yes	Yes	No	Yes	No	Yes	Yes	$20	June–Sept
Lodgepole	6,700	214	0	Yes	Yes	Yes	Yes	Yes	Yes		Yes	$18–$20	All year
Potwisha	2,100	42	0	Yes	Yes	Yes	No	Yes	No	Yes	No	$18	All year
South Fork	3,600	10	0	No	Yes	No	No	Yes	No	No	No	$12	All year
INSIDE KINGS CANYON NATIONAL PARK													
Azalea	6,500	113	0	No	Yes	Yes	Yes	Yes	No	Yes	No	$18	All year
Crystal Springs	6,500	62	0	No	Yes	Yes	Yes	Yes	No	Yes	No	$18	May–Sept
Moraine	4,600	120	0	No	Yes	Yes	Yes	Yes	Yes	Yes	No	$18	May–Oct
Sentinel	4,600	82	0	No	Yes	Yes	Yes	Yes	Yes	Yes	No	$18	Apr–Oct
Sheep Creek	4,600	111	0	No	Yes	Yes	Yes	Yes	Yes	Yes	No	$14	June–Nov
Sunset	6,500	200	0	No	Yes	Yes	Yes	Yes	Yes	No	No	$18	May–Sept

OUTSIDE THE PARKS													
Big Meadows	7,600	30	0	No	Yes	No	No	Yes	No	Yes	No	Free	May–Oct
Hume Lake	5,200	74	0	No	Yes	Yes	No	Yes	No	Yes	Yes	$17–$19	May–Oct
Landslide	5,800	9	0	No	Yes	No	No	Yes	No	No	No	$13–$15	May–Oct
Princess	5,900	88	0	Yes	Yes	Yes	No	Yes	No	No	Yes	$15–$17	May–Oct
Stony Creek	6,400	49	0	No	Yes	Yes	Yes	Yes	No	Yes	Yes	$17–$19	May–Oct
Tenmile	5,800	13	0	No	Yes	Yes	No	Yes	No	No	No	$13–$15	May–Oct
Horse Creek	300	80	0	Yes	Yes	Yes	Yes	Yes	No	Yes	Yes	$16	All year
Lemon Cove	500	55	40	Yes	Yes	Yes	Yes	Yes	Yes	Yes	Yes	$22–$30	All year

Creek, located along picturesque Sheep Creek, is generally open on an as-needed basis.

OUTSIDE THE PARKS

The U.S. Forest Service operates a number of campgrounds in **Giant Sequoia National Monument,** a 327,769-acre section of Sequoia National Forest, which was given national monument status by U.S. President Bill Clinton in April 2000. These sites provide a delightful forest camping experience and are usually less crowded than the national park campgrounds. For information, contact **Giant Sequoia National Monument,** Sequoia National Forest, Hume Lake Ranger District, 35860 E. Kings Canyon Rd., Dunlap, CA 93621 (© **559/ 338-2251;** fax 559/338-2131; www.r5.fs.fed.us/sequoia).

In the Hume Lake area, all the forest service campgrounds have pit toilets except the beautiful **Hume Lake Campground,** which is set on the banks of the lake and has flush toilets. It's about 3 miles south of CA 180 via Hume Lake Road. The largest campground in this area is **Princess,** located along CA 180. Two smaller campgrounds, both beyond Hume Lake via Ten Mile Road, are **Landslide** and **Upper Ten Mile.**

In the Stony Creek/Big Meadows area, you'll find vault toilets at all U.S. Forest Service campgrounds except **Stony Creek Campground,** located off Generals Highway in Stony Creek Village, which has flush toilets. Among the larger campgrounds in this area is **Big Meadows,** which is set along Big Meadows Creek. Nearby trails lead to the Jennie Lakes Wilderness. From Grant Grove Village, drive 7 miles southeast on the Generals Highway, then turn east on Big Meadows Road and drive 5 miles to the campground. There are also several smaller, primitive campgrounds here; you can get information about them from the U.S. Forest Service (see above).

You can make reservations at Hume Lake, Princess, or Stony Creek during the summer by calling © **877/444-6777** or visiting **www. reserveusa.com.**

Another great place to camp is **Horse Creek Campground,** operated by the U.S. Army Corps of Engineers. It's located along the south shore of Lake Kaweah, in Lake Kaweah Recreation Area, about 6 miles east of the community of Lemon Cove off CA 198. The lake, which is about 5 miles long and a half-mile wide, covers 1,900 acres when full and is popular with boaters, who take to the water in kayaks, canoes, personal watercraft, fishing boats, and larger patio boats. There are several boat ramps, and boat rentals are available at the **Kaweah Marina** (© **559/597-2526**). Call for current rates and availability. This is also a popular fishing lake, where you're apt to catch largemouth bass, crappie, bluegill, catfish, and rainbow trout. The number of campsites varies with the water level, with the fewest usually in spring, when the lake is at its highest; many sites are underwater here until mid-July. Some are shady sites and some open, and most have good views across the lake. The campground has flush toilets. For information, contact **U.S. Army Corps of Engineers,** Lake Kaweah Recreation Area, P.O. Box 44270, Lemon Cove, CA 93244 (© 559/597-2301). Campsite reservations are available from the National Recreation Reservation Service (© 877/444-7275; www. reserveamerica.com).

Those seeking a full-service commercial campground with RV hookups and all the usual amenities should head to **Lemon Cove/Sequoia Campground,** on the west side of Lemon Cove at 32075 Sierra Dr., P.O. Box 44269, Lemon Cove, CA 93244 (© 559/ 597-2346; www.lemoncovesequoiacamp.com). This attractive and convenient campground (22 miles east of U.S. 99), located in the foothills of the Sierra Nevada, can handle large rigs with slide-outs and offers cable TV hookups, propane sales, a convenience store, grassy and shaded sites, a recreation room, a playground and volleyball court, and an outdoor swimming pool.

3 Where to Eat

Major improvements and additions to the restaurant scene in these parks in recent years mean that, yes, you can have a really good meal, or, if you prefer, find a quick and tasty lunch at a fairly reasonable price. In addition, there are several good possibilities in the communities outside the park and within the Giant Sequoia National Monument.

IN THE PARK

Every Wednesday through Sunday from mid-June to early September, **"Dinner with a Ranger"** takes place in the beautiful outdoor setting of Wolverton Meadow, just south of Lodgepole in Sequoia, featuring an all-you-can-eat barbecue followed by an interpretive program such as a campfire sing-a-long, meadow nature walk, or wildlife talk. The cost is $18.95 for adults and $9.95 for children 12 and under. Tickets can be purchased at the Wuksachi Lodge or Lodgepole Market. Call © 559/253-2199 for information. There is also a **pizzeria** at Stony Creek Lodge on Generals Highway between Grant Grove and Wuksachi (© 559/452-1081) that serves lunch and dinner.

Cedar Grove Café AMERICAN   Providing the only dining at Cedar Grove, this glorified snack bar offers a simple but adequate menu at affordable prices, although those staying at the lodge here for several days will quickly tire of the limited choices. The cafe has a pleasant outdoor balcony seating area that overlooks the river.

Cedar Grove, Kings Canyon National Park. Breakfast $4–$9; lunch and dinner $5–$15. AE, DISC, MC, V. Mid-June to early Sept daily 7am–2pm, 5–9pm; early Sept to mid-Oct Mon–Fri 8–10:30am, Sat–Sun 8am–2pm, daily 5–7pm. Closed mid-Oct to mid-June.

Grant Grove Restaurant ☙ *Kids* AMERICAN   This pleasant cafe-style restaurant, located in the hub of activity in Kings Canyon National Park, is the primary option for a sit-down meal, with a simple but very adequate menu and good service. Breakfast and lunch are typical American fare, including pizza—always a favorite with kids. Complete dinners include steaks, pastas, chicken, and tasty trout dishes.

Grant Grove Village, Kings Canyon National Park. Breakfast and lunch $4–$10; dinner $7–$24. AE, DISC, MC, V. May–Aug daily 7am–9pm; Sept–Apr daily 7am–8pm.

Lodgepole Deli & Snack Bar ☙ *Value* DELI/PIZZA   The deli and the snack bar are actually two separate counter-service, fast-food restaurants in the Lodgepole Market Center. At the snack bar, you'll find kids' favorites such as burgers, hot dogs, and pizza. Healthier grown-up fare is available at the deli, which specializes in made-to-order deli-style sandwiches, wraps, and salads—and ice cream.

Lodgepole, Sequoia National Park. ✆ 559/565-3301. Most items $3–$7. AE, MC, V. Daily 8am–8pm. Snack bar open year-round with shorter hours fall–spring; deli closed Nov–Apr.

Wuksachi Dining Room ☙☙ AMERICAN   A high, natural wood–beamed ceiling; huge stone fireplace; and large windows offering wonderful views of the surrounding forest make this upscale mountain-lodge–style restaurant a delightful spot for a refined and relaxing meal. Standard American breakfasts are the morning fare, and a number of salads and sandwiches—such as a half-pound burger or citrus-marinated salmon with caramelized onion—are offered during lunch and dinner. The main dinner entrees are quite elegant. We recommend the lavender chicken, with honey-roasted shallots and balsamic syrup; the rib-eye steak, served with portobello-ancho sauce; or for those who can't decide, the triple divide plate, which includes a filet mignon smothered in a sauce of black beans and chiles, plus a chicken breast and grilled shrimp.

Wuksachi Lodge, Sequoia National Park. © 559/565-4070, ext. 608. Dinner reservations required. Sandwiches and salads $4–$9; Dinner entrees $13–$25. AE, DISC, MC, V. Daily 7–10am, 11:30am–2pm, and 5–10pm.

OUTSIDE THE PARKS

Anne Lang's Emporium DELI   A great spot for a quick lunch or to pick up a picnic lunch before heading into the park. This busy, full-service deli has a half-dozen or so small tables inside, in a cafe-like atmosphere, plus a large deck out back (away from the highway) that overlooks the Kaweah River. You order at the counter, and the staff will prepare your sandwich to eat there or as a box lunch. In addition to the usual cold deli sandwiches, there are a few hot items, including burgers and chicken-breast sandwiches. There are also several luncheon salads, a soup of the day, fresh baked items, ice cream, and specialty drinks including espressos, smoothies, and Italian sodas.

41651 Sierra Dr. (CA 198), Three Rivers. © 559/561-4937. Most items $2.95–$5.95. MC, V. Mon–Fri 10am–4pm; Sat–Sun 11am–4pm.

Hummingbirds *Finds* AMERICAN   A friendly, folksy, family-run restaurant, Hummingbirds offers hearty, homemade grub, from freshly baked cornbread and rolls to juicy burgers and steaks, seafood, pasta, and other traditional plates. Breakfasts are dominated by eggs, potatoes, and ham—try the country eggs Benedict if you've got a day of hiking and need that extra fuel. The desserts make the place, all made in house from scratch, including peach cobbler, cakes, and delectable blackberry pies.

35591 E. Kings Canyon Rd., Clingan's Junction (19 miles west of the Kings Canyon NP boundary). © 559/338-0160. Menu items $4.25–$15. AE, MC, V. Daily 7:30am–8:30pm.

River View AMERICAN   A favorite for bikers from near and far, the River View is actually a pretty good place for just about anybody to grab a good meal and watch the Kaweah River rush by. There's a popular bar inside and a great deck outside, and plenty to look at in either spot. The menu runs the gamut from hot sandwiches and juicy burgers to T-bones and salmon dinners to pizzas, with a side of live music on weekends. If you're looking to have a few beers and unwind, this is just the ticket.

42323 Sierra Dr., Three Rivers. © 559/561-2211. Sandwiches and burgers $5–$7.50, dinner main courses $11.50–$23.50, pizzas $8 and up. AE, DISC, MC, V. Sun–Thurs 10:30am–9pm; Fri–Sat 10:30am–10pm. Bar open later.

Vintage Press 🎔🎔🎔 *Finds* AMERICAN/CONTINENTAL   The best place to eat within miles, this is our choice for celebrating a special occasion or just giving ourselves a treat. The restaurant's three dining rooms are all somewhat different, but all are elegant in the spirit of an upscale gin mill in Gold Rush–era San Francisco. There is a handsome old bar imported from the city by the bay, and many antiques and leaded mirrors. There is also patio dining. The menu features a dozen meat and fish selections, including steak; free-range chicken with braised leeks; and crispy veal sweetbreads with a port wine–jalapeño-blue cheese sauce. Those who want a somewhat lighter meal or who desire to experience this fine restaurant at a slightly lower cost, can make a dinner of one of the exotic appetizers ($8.95–$12), or come for lunch (steaks, pastas, and salads). The restaurant's wine cellar, a winner of the *Wine Spectator* Award of Excellence, offers over 1,000 selections.

216 N. Willis St., Visalia. (℃ 559/733-3033. Reservations recommended at dinner. Main courses $9–$14 lunch, $16–$33 dinner. AE, DC, MC, V. Mon–Thurs 11:30am–2pm and 5:30–10pm; Fri–Sat 11:30am–2pm and 5:30–10:30pm; Sun brunch 10:30am–2pm, Sun dinner 5–9pm.

FOR PICNIC & CAMPING SUPPLIES

Stores throughout the parks stock some basic camping supplies, such as flashlights, canteens, and tarps, and enough food that you won't starve, but you'll find better selections in the nearby towns.

Within the parks, most of the stores are open daily from 8am until 7 or 8pm. The **Cedar Grove Market** is open May through September only, as is the **Lodgepole Market,** which has the widest selection available, including a good deli for takeout sandwiches (see above). The **Grant Grove Market** is open from 8am to 9pm May through August and from 8am to 7pm September through April. During the winter a small variety of goods are available at **Wuksachi Lodge,** in Sequoia.

For the best selection and prices on foodstuffs outside the parks, stop in Visalia at **Save Mart,** in the Mary's Vineyard Shopping Center at CA 198 and Ben Maddox Way on your way to the parks. This is an excellent supermarket with a good bakery and a deli that serves made-to-order sandwiches. Just east of Mary's Vineyard Shopping Center is a **Wal-Mart** discount store, at 1819 E. Noble Ave., where you'll find a wide stock of camping supplies, along with film, clothing, and practically everything else you might need.

9

A Nature Guide to Yosemite and Sequoia & Kings Canyon National Parks

Yosemite and Sequoia & Kings Canyon are parks in transition. Both have long been geologic wonderlands, rarities that recently ran headlong into myriad social concerns and natural disasters. Now park enthusiasts, rangers, and the National Park Service are all taking a serious look at the parks' futures.

1 The Landscape

Towering sheets of granite. Lush forests that give way to emerald meadows blanketed in wildflowers. Views that stretch longer than some countries and make visitors feel like they are standing on the edge of the world. The landscape throughout these parks is memorable. Yosemite has an almost bizarre conglomeration of sheer granite monoliths and wide-open spaces. Sequoia & Kings Canyon has trees that are as wide at the base as some homes, and wildflowers in almost every patch of sun. All these wonders occur because of the area's astounding geological nature.

About 300 million years ago, layers of sediment that had been building up on the ocean floor were forced under the emerging North American continent. The process created such intense heat that the sediment became molten lava (magma), some of which erupted into volcanoes. Where it chilled and hardened before reaching the surface, the magma created huge slabs of granite.

This process continued intermittently for about 150 million years, forming a large mountain range roughly parallel to the West Coast— the Sierra Nevada. For the next 55 million years, wind and water ate away at the volcanoes and sedimentary rock, sweeping it into California's Central Valley and leaving mountains of exposed granite.

Scientists theorize that 25 million years ago, earthquakes along the present-day San Andreas Fault began forcing the eastern edge of a landmass beneath the Sierra upward, eventually tipping west, raising tall mountain peaks. In Yosemite, the upheaval raised the park's eastern range to 11,000 feet, and in Sequoia & Kings Canyon, it created the ominously barren and beautiful Kaweah Ridge, also known as the Great Western Divide, which ranges from about 10,900 to 13,600 feet in elevation.

As rivers raged through the valleys, they continued to carve deeper into the earth, eroding the bedrock. Great canyons were formed, and when the earth's temperature cooled, 2 to 3 million years ago, glaciers covered the Sierra Nevada. These fields of ice tore at the granite, expanding and contracting with such force that they carved deep valleys, slicing granite walls vertically into the steep U-shape of Yosemite Valley and Kings Canyon.

When the glaciers melted, they left behind steep mountains smoothed by ice, and piles of debris that dammed the flow of rivers, creating lakes in the valleys. The rest of the landscaping took place in an evolutionary blink of an eye. Over the course of 10,000 years, sediment, swept down from above, filled these lakes. Meadows were formed; then came wildflowers, followed by trees, and eventually people.

You can still see glaciers in Yosemite, up near Tuolumne Meadows. Also check out the glaciers on Yosemite's Mount Lyell, Mount Dana, and Mount Maclure. The glaciers here were probably formed 2,500 years ago and are quickly receding.

Glaciers are responsible for the variety of rock formations in the parks. There are spires, domes, sheets, and arches. Yosemite has cornered the market for number and diversity, offering one or more of each within the span of an easy 3-mile walk. Most of the unusual rock landmarks here were created by fractures within the rock. These fractures occur vertically, horizontally, and at an incline. Called *joints,* they represent the weakest point of a rock and a point that has already been broken. The type of joint most common in Yosemite, and also evident in Sequoia & Kings Canyon, is sheeting. Concentric joints—fractures that seem to occur along curved lines—form after years of increasing and decreasing pressure from overlaying rock. When pressure decreases, the granite expands upward and breaks or fractures off in sheets, similar to peeling an onion very slowly.

Erratic boulders are another common sight. These large rocks were originally located elsewhere but were transported and plopped down haphazardly—again, probably by glaciers.

Ridges of rocky deposits are called *moraines,* left behind as glaciers recede. The best place to see moraines is in Yosemite, en route from Tuolumne Meadows to Tioga Pass.

The most famous rocks in Yosemite are Half Dome and El Capitan. Although Half Dome was probably never a full dome like North Dome, which it faces, geologists believe that about 20% of the original rock was sheared off by glaciers. The face looks smooth and slippery but is actually filled with ledges and ridges, making it a rock climber's paradise. Similar ridges exist on the dome side, enabling hikers to climb to the top (see chapter 4). Although it looks small, the top measures 13 acres. Half Dome is 8,842 feet above sea level and towers roughly 4,800 feet above the valley floor, the highest point in Yosemite Valley.

El Capitan is on the left, or north, side of the valley as you enter. It rises 3,593 feet above the valley floor and 7,569 feet above sea level. Toward the top of El Cap, the slope of the rock actually increases and hangs over the valley floor. Called the *nose,* it's a particular challenge for rock climbers. Look for climbers on the face, as well as off to the sides of El Cap; it's where many experts ascend and beginners learn the ropes. It takes 5 to 8 days to climb El Capitan. The first climber reached the summit in 1958, after 43 days. The rock is also home to a pair of peregrine falcons that nest here in spring and summer.

To the east of El Cap are the Three Brothers—three outcroppings of rock called Lower Brother, Middle Brother, and Eagle Peak. The rocks appear to be riding piggyback and were formed by parallel fractures on an incline.

The Cathedral Spires are directly opposite El Cap, on the other side of the valley. They will appear before you if you turn your back to El Cap and look carefully—the rock is almost camouflaged by the valley wall beyond. Somehow these, and other spires in the park, have withstood nature's evolutionary barrage.

Another spire, this one known as Lost Arrow, is east of Yosemite Falls, below Yosemite Point. Look for the waterfalls to the north of Yosemite Lodge. The outcropping of rock to the east is Yosemite Point. Lost Arrow is an independent spire in the same area.

Continue moving east to see the Royal Arches, a series of 1,500-foot half circles carved out of the rock, to the north of The Ahwahnee Hotel. The Arches provide an inside view of the exfoliation process that formed many of Yosemite's domes. Here, the material that was once above the arches eroded away, taking pressure off the rock below, which expanded and cracked parallel to the surface.

During particularly wet springs, water cascades over the arches in great sheets.

Above the arches is North Dome, the smooth, slightly lopsided dome mentioned above. It rises 3,562 feet above the valley floor. Nearby is Washington Column, a spire with a tip 1,920 feet above the valley floor. Ahwahnee Indian legend has it that a man and woman who lived in the valley long ago fought so often that it upset the spirits. The unhappy couple was turned to stone and separated by Tenaya Creek. He is North Dome, with Washington Column as his walking stick. She is Half Dome, and if you look at it closely, a woman's profile faces northeast. Legend also has it that the streak of lighter rock between her cheek and nose was caused by a stream of tears.

Domes and impressive geologic formations appear outside the valley as well. Most are in Yosemite's high country, en route to Tuolumne Meadows, and foremost is Olmsted Point, an overlook that gives visitors a chance to see the granite Tenaya Canyon. Cloud's Rest and the rear of Half Dome are two distinct shapes easily recognizable from Olmsted Point, which is 9 miles west of Tuolumne Meadows.

Tuolumne Meadows itself is ringed with domes and peaks, many of which are an easier climb than the ones rising above the valley.

In Sequoia, Moro Rock is a dome towering 6,725 feet above sea level. Moro Rock's summit offers breathtaking views of the Kaweah Ridge, with some peaks rising to 14,000 feet.

Kings Canyon boasts North Dome, above Cedar Grove. Some people with a vivid imagination say it resembles Half Dome. North Dome is not accessible by car or on foot.

Waterfalls hang over the Yosemite Valley like a sparkling diamond necklace. The valley boasts three of the world's tallest waterfalls. Upon entering the valley, you'll spot the 620-foot Bridalveil Fall first. It looks large, but that's because you haven't seen the rest of the cast.

The real biggie is Yosemite Falls, close to Yosemite Lodge. The fall appears to be one drop but is, in fact, a set of waterfalls that measures a combined 2,425 feet. Lower Yosemite Fall drops 320 feet; Upper Yosemite Fall descends 1,430 feet; and a cascade in the middle makes up the difference.

To the west of El Capitan you'll find Ribbon Fall, which drops an uninterrupted 1,612 feet to the valley floor but is often dry in summer.

The longest single fall in Yosemite is Sentinel Fall. It drops 2,000 feet from the west side of Sentinel Rock, directly across the valley floor from Yosemite Falls. To view this waterfall, walk back toward

Fun Fact The Life and Times of John Muir

Few people have loved the Sierra Nevada like John Muir, before or since. In the late 19th century, he pushed for conservation of the pristine wilderness and then helped establish both Yosemite and Sequoia & Kings Canyon as National Parks.

Born in Scotland in 1838, Muir emigrated with his family to Wisconsin at the age of 11. About a decade later, he dropped everything and decided to go to the Amazon—on foot. He didn't make it, but traveling became a way of life for Muir and his journeys eventually took him West. He discovered the Sierra Nevada area in 1868 and worked as a shepherd in the Yosemite area. He later ran a sawmill nearby.

Muir began writing about the Sierra Nevada from pretty much the moment he arrived, and his passionate words started finding an audience in the late 19th-century United States. He wrote a number of books, contributed to numerous periodicals, and became a leading voice in the budding environmentalist movement. In 1892, Muir helped found the Sierra Club. In 1903, he took Teddy Roosevelt camping in the Yosemite backcountry and catalyzed T. R.'s vision of an entire system of national parks.

Muir is a legend for not only his words and his deeds, but also because he was something of an eccentric. He never shaved, making way for quite the impressive beard. He experienced nature to its fullest—meaning he climbed a tree during an incredible storm, sledded down Yosemite Valley's steep walls on his rump to avoid an avalanche, and chased a bear so he could study the animal's stride. (*Note:* These actions have since been banned by the National Park Service.)

From the first moment a politician pondered Hetch Hetchy Reservoir, Muir fought it. Damming and drowning a place whose beauty rivaled that of Yosemite Valley was sacrilege to him. But San Francisco needed water to drink, and Congress passed legislation approving Hetch Hetchy Reservoir in 1913. John Muir died the very next year, some say of a broken heart.

El Cap and make an about-face—it's one of the geology-obscured views in the park.

Up the valley are a series of dramatic staircase falls accessible only on foot. Vernal and Nevada falls occur just a half mile apart along the same river.

Waterfalls in Sequoia & Kings Canyon are less numerous but still impressive. Mist Falls in Kings Canyon is beautiful but requires a 4-mile hike (see chapter 7). This wide waterfall near Cedar Grove is up a rushing creek, which includes several large cascades.

Below is Roaring River Falls, a length of waterfall also accessible only on foot, which flows from Cloud and Deadman canyons. Garlic Falls, in the Monarch Wilderness area just outside Kings Canyon, can be viewed from the Yucca Point overlook on CA 180.

A note on waterfalls: Most are fed by snowmelt and rely on winter runoff to survive. In late summer, many of them (including Yosemite Falls) dry up.

2 The Flora

There are more than 1,500 types of plants in Yosemite and Sequoia & Kings Canyon, and describing them all would fill this book. With species ranging from tiny lichen to giant sequoias, the flora in both parks is similar, varying primarily by elevation.

TREES

The trees native to the region consist mostly of conifers and broadleaf trees. Conifers have needles and cones, do not shed during cooler months, and maintain their green year-round, earning the name *evergreen.* Broadleaf trees drop their leaves in fall and bloom anew in spring.

At lower elevations, the two most common pines you'll find are the ponderosa pine and Jeffrey pine (both also known as "yellow pines"). **Ponderosa pines** have yellow-orange bark, needles grouped in threes, and bark scales that fit together like a jigsaw puzzle. The trunk of a ponderosa pine can grow up to 6 feet in diameter. The **Jeffrey pine** is similar to the ponderosa but tends to live at higher elevations.

Sugar pines grow at slightly higher elevations and can be seen along many hikes. These pines produce large pinecones, have short needles grouped in fives, and have a reddish-brown bark. Trunks can grow to almost 7 feet in diameter, and mature trees sport very crooked branches.

Ponderosa Pine

Jeffrey Pine

Pines found at higher elevations include the lodgepole and white-bark. **Lodgepole pines,** the most widely distributed pine in North America, group their needles in twos, and have yellow-orange bark and small cones. **Whitebark pines** bunch five needles together and have sticky purple-tinted cones. These pines tend to be smaller, and are found closer to the tree line.

Sugar Pine

Lodgepole Pine

Firs are another species of conifer found in the parks. **Red firs**—with short needles that curl up, and cones ranging from 5 to 8 inches—are found at elevations of 6,000 to 9,000 feet. **White firs,** found at lower elevations from about 3,500 to 8,000 feet, have 2-inch needles that grow in twists off the branch, grayish bark, and 3- to 5-inch cones. Old trunks frequently form large cavities at the base and are used by wildlife as refuges. Both firs grow in forests near Yosemite's Glacier Point and in the high country along Tioga Road. White firs can be seen throughout Sequoia & Kings Canyon.

At the highest elevations (9,000 ft.–14,000 ft.), look for **foxtail pines,** gnarled trees that have adapted to the harsh rocky life of living at the top. This pine, like the whitebark pine, looks stunted and warped, often with a twisted trunk and spiky, dead-looking top. The roots grow over granite and require only a short growing season, allowing the tree to cling to a frigid existence.

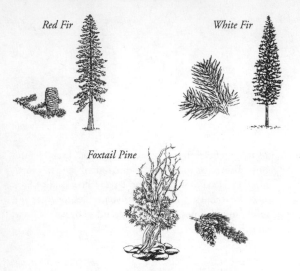

Red Fir

White Fir

Foxtail Pine

The uncommon **California nutmeg** resembles a fir, with sharp single needles, and can be found along the Marble Fork Trail in Sequoia National Park as you near a creek flowing over marble slabs. **Incense cedar** is often confused with the giant sequoias, as both have reddish shaggy bark that almost crumbles to the touch. But an incense cedar has flat sprays of foliage that emit a fragrant smell in warm weather, and small reddish-brown cones resembling a duck's bill when opened.

The undisputed heavyweight of the national parks' flora is the **giant sequoia.** Smaller ones can be hard to identify, but there is no mistaking a mature 250-foot tree dating back 2,000 to 3,000 years. These trees grow to a height of 311 feet, weigh 2.7 million pounds, and can have a base 40 feet in diameter. Tree limbs can reach 8 feet in diameter. The trees are bare until about 100 to 150 feet up, and then sprout branches. The bark, naturally fire resistant, ranges from 4 to 24 inches thick. These trees are resistant to decay, and they produce abundant small cones with hundreds of seeds the size of oatmeal flakes. Interestingly, it takes a fire to dry the cones out enough to release the seeds.

Incense cedar

Giant Sequoia

Giant sequoias can be found at elevations ranging from 5,000 to 7,500 feet, and occasionally as low as 3,500 feet. Obviously, the best place to see these trees is throughout Sequoia & Kings Canyon National Parks. The large stands of Giant Forest and Grant Grove offer fantastic, easily accessible examples of giant sequoias, and there are other groves, accessible by foot, scattered throughout the park. Yosemite has three stands of giant sequoias—the Mariposa Grove near Wawona, and the smaller Tuolumne and Merced groves near the Big Oak Flat Entrance.

Broadleaf trees in the area include the **California black oak,** which grows at lower elevations in both parks. The dark gray to black bark of these trees is distinctive. They also produce acorns and can grow to a height of 75 feet. **Blue oaks** lose their leaves in fall, and can be found in foothills of 1,000 to 5,000 feet elevation. Hollylike evergreen leaves mark the **canyon live oak,** the other common oak tree in the region.

The **Pacific dogwood** produces blooms with whitish-green flowers each spring. The **quaking aspen** has paper-thin white bark and an army of small leaves that rustle in the slightest wind. Along streams and rivers at lower elevations, look for cottonwoods, willows, and alders.

Canyon Live Oak

FLOWERING PLANTS

Wildflowers produce an array of colors during spring and summer, as they peek from cracks and crevices or carpet fields and meadows. The blooming season begins in February in the lowlands, and lasts into early fall in the high country. The list of wildflowers found in these parks is intimidating and includes more than 50 species, some of which are described below.

Splashed on meadows and along hillsides is a lavender flower, **lupine.** It's easily recognized by palmate leaves—leaves that originate from a central point like fingers from a hand. Look for the bloom along valley floors and in the Wawona region of Yosemite. You will also see **cow parsnip** here, bluish-tinged flowers set on spindly stems, with almost fernlike leaves. The cow parsnip's dart-like flowers resemble violets at a distance, but closer inspection reveals an umbrella-shaped top and leafless stalk. Large blue-to-purple blooms that shoot out amid tall, narrow leaves are **wild irises.** In the Wawona region of Yosemite, look for **mountain misery,** clumps of small, white flowers atop fluffy, pine-needle-looking leaves; and **farewell-to-spring,** a whimsical pinkish flower with four large, fragile petals and small, slender leaves.

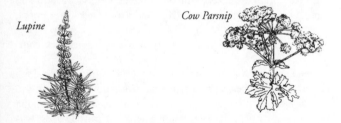

Lupine

Cow Parsnip

You may also see monkey flower, showy milkweed, and yarrow at these elevations. **Monkey flower** is one of nature's brightest flowers, ranging from blue to purple, pink, and orange, and seen along streams and at high altitudes in gravelly soil. Petals consist of two-lipped blossoms that more imaginative folk say resemble the smiling face of a monkey. **Showy milkweed** grows in meadows and forest clearings. These sturdy plants have large oval-shaped leaves and stocks filled with a poisonous milky sap. In summer, colorful bunches of tiny five-petal flowers appear; later the milkweed pods burst, releasing a tuft of silky seeds to scatter in the wind. **Yarrow** blooms as a flat, wide cluster of white (occasionally pink) flowers with a pungent aroma. Growing up to 3 feet tall, it was used by Native Americans as a healing herb, a drink to cure indigestion and to reduce fever. Today, the dried flower is commonly seen in potpourri.

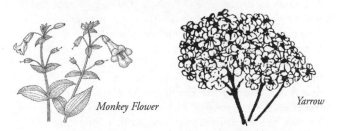

Monkey Flower

Yarrow

At night, look for **evening primrose**—its four-petal flowers open at sunset and wilt in the morning, and are pollinated by moths. Blossoms range from white to yellow and pink and have a sweet lemon smell; stems can reach 6 feet.

One of the last flowers of the season is **meadow goldenrod,** which appears in late summer and fall. The plant grows in long stalks, with narrow leaves protruding all along it, and may be topped by a shock of yellow that resembles a feather. Goldenrod was used by American Indians to cure all sorts of ailments.

Evening Primrose

Meadow Goldenrod

In forests, you'll find pussy paws and snow plant in the shade, and lupine, the Mariposa lily, and mountain violet in the sun. The **snow plant** has a flaming red or orange stalk, while **pussy paws** have small, fuzzy leaves and delicate flowers that group together to resemble the shape of a cat's paw. The **Mariposa lily,** which blooms beneath pines in Yosemite, is named for the Spanish word for butterfly, which it is said to resemble. Blooms consist of three snow-white petals with dark spots at their base; the long stems give the flowers a floating appearance. American Indians roasted the bulbs of these blooms to eat.

Mariposa Lily

At higher and cooler elevations, a number of slender blooms abound. The **mountain sorrel** has leaves shaped like lilies, and clusters of small pink flowers no bigger than the tip of a fingernail. **Spreading phlox** has pointed leaves that stick out like thorns and broad, flat flowers on top. The **meadow penstemon** produces a group of bright pink flowers atop a single slender stalk. The blooms are arranged like trumpets, pointing in every direction.

Mountain Sorrel   *Meadow Penstemon*

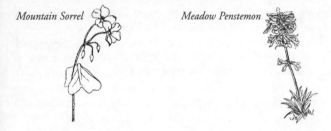

Columbine grows in meadows and springs from rocky crevices. A favorite flower of hummingbirds, columbine looks quite fragile, with bushy leaves clumped at the base of bare stalks that produce droopy blooms. Their color can vary, but look for five petals that extend backward in a long, pointed tube.

Columbine

SHRUBS & PLANTS

One of the many plants found in the parks is the wild azalea. These plants resemble their household cousins and are often the first to proclaim the arrival of spring, with an abundance of vibrant color. The Sierra sports just one variety: the **western azalea,** a low-lying shrub with smooth, deep-green leaves.

Western Azalea

Bear clover is a low-growing shrub with sticky leaves and a pungent smell, found in the Lodgepole area of Sequoia and at elevations around 7,000 to 8,000 feet.

The **Mariposa manzanita,** with its smooth red-to-purple bark and oval, coin-size leaves, blooms year-round and is but one type of manzanita common in this region. The Mariposa manzanita produces small white and pink clusters of flowers that eventually turn into berries that look like little apples, which is what *manzanita* means in Spanish. This shrub is plentiful in the foothills of Sequoia National Park.

Mariposa Manzanita

Now look up into oak trees and search for a clump of green bush that looks as if it were growing out of branches. This is **mistletoe.** Despite its holiday charm, it is a parasite more than a shrub, growing in green bunches high up in the treetops and sucking nourishment from oaks and other trees. Another pest is **poison oak,** prevalent below 5,000 feet. Watch for a shrub with shiny three-leaf clusters and white berries. In winter, poison oak stems are bare and very difficult to recognize, so steer clear of any thickets that resemble sticks stuck in the ground.

Poison Oak

3 The Fauna

Think of the parks as nature's zoo. There are no cages, no man-made habitats—just wide-open spaces with enough room for more than 200 species of mammals and birds, some of which are described below.

BIRDS

The Sierra Nevada is a bird-watcher's paradise. Each year, 135 species visit Yosemite Valley alone. The most treasured of the area's feathered friends include the great horned owl, the peregrine falcon, and the California condor, all of which send bird-watchers into ornithological ecstasy. You're more likely to hear the **great horned owl** than see one. Its hoots sound like sonar, but since it is nocturnal, it's difficult to spot. If you happen to hear it, try to locate its branch first, and then the bird: It has large tufts of feathers near both ears. But don't get disheartened if you search in vain—these birds are great ventriloquists. You'll have more luck observing a pair of nesting **peregrine falcons** on El Capitan or Glacier Point, although you'll need binoculars. For several years now, a number of pairs have made this their own personal day-care center, hatching and raising their young on narrow ledges before beginning flight instruction. One of four falcon species in the park, the peregrine falcon is marked by a hood of dark feathers from head to back, contrasting against lighter ones underneath. This bird is a wizard in flight, reaching speeds of up to 200 mph mid-dive. It's an endangered species.

Great Horned Owl

Peregrine Falcon

Also endangered is the **California condor,** the largest land bird in North America, with a 9-foot wingspan. The birds are able to glide 10 miles at a time without flapping their wings. Keen eyesight allows them to spot a dead animal carcass from miles away. Their numbers dropped below 40 in 1975, due to pesticide use and the loss of habitat to building . A pair of condors can raise only one young every 2 years. In the 1980s, the remaining birds were captured and placed in zoos where young were hand-reared. Then some of the adolescent birds were released into the wild and have been seen in Kings Canyon.

California Condor

In both parks, the birds you're most likely to see are the American robin, Steller's jay, acorn woodpecker, northern flicker, band-tailed pigeon, two varieties of blackbird, sparrow, swift, American dipper, belted kingfisher, duck, warbler, brown creeper, mountain chickadee, and red-breasted and white-breasted nuthatches. Yosemite Valley is a great place to see many of these species because its environment includes streambeds, rivers, forest, and meadowlands, often within the space of a city block. A stroll anywhere along the Merced River should take you within visual distance of all of these birds, whose habitats include the water, meadows, and adjacent forests.

A reddish-orange breast easily distinguishes the **American robin.** These are the same birds you can see back home throughout much of North America, in suburbs and backyards, building cup-shaped nests on windowsills or the ledges of buildings. Before the bird adapted to urban living, it preferred a woodland habitat. It has long been considered a harbinger of spring, but in reality some of these birds stay put year-round. The **Steller's jay** is one of nature's more annoying birds. Unfazed by humans, it is a bold beggar, landing on picnic tables and elsewhere near food, while letting loose a screech that could wake the dead. The Steller's jay is bright blue, with a dark head and prominent crest. This bird is also capable of a beautiful soft warble.

American Robin

Steller's Jay

Like the Steller's jay, you're likely to hear the **woodpecker** before you see it—listen for its methodical rata-tat-tat. Woodpeckers can also emit a startling call that sounds like "wack-up." Woodpeckers are distinguished by black-and-white markings and a red crown, with an occasional bit of yellow. The **northern flicker** is also a woodpecker—look for a brown-feathered bird clinging to the side of a tree. Its wings have a reddish tinge and it sports a red mustache. This bird prefers to feed on the ground, where it searches for ants. **Band-tailed pigeons** are similar to their city-dwelling cousins but prefer tall forest trees to buildings.

Northern Flicker

Band-tailed Pigeon

In meadowlands, you will likely see sparrows, the black-headed grosbeak, the uncommon western tanager—a bird with fluorescent feathers—and two varieties of blackbird. The **Brewer's blackbird** and the **red-winged blackbird** both make their home here. Brewer's blackbirds nest in trees, while their red-winged relatives prefer slightly marshy areas. Red-winged males have distinctive red patches on their wings. The Brewer's blackbird is, well, black, and females of either variety are drab in comparison to the males. **Sparrows** are small singing birds, streaked by brown feathers and with cone-shaped beaks. Their babies leave the nest 10 days after birth. The **black-headed grosbeak** has black, white, and orange markings, and a distinctive beak used for cracking seeds. Its soft, lyrical warble is music compared to other valley dwellers, and this bird is considered a sure sign of spring. The easy-to-spot **western tanager** is bright yellow with a reddish-orange head and is frequently observed in Yosemite Valley during spring and summer.

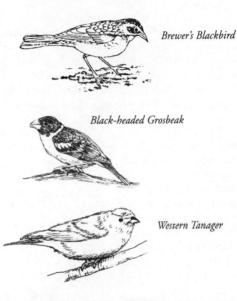

Brewer's Blackbird

Black-headed Grosbeak

Western Tanager

If you're near moving water, you might search for **American dippers,** belted kingfishers, ducks, and warblers. The dipper is notable more for its flying acrobatics than for its nondescript color. The bird flies headfirst into the river to walk upstream along the bottom, clinging to rocks in its search for food. The **belted kingfisher** is a highly visible blue bird that flies low over water in search of prey. You may see it perched above the water, clinging to branches and underbrush, and keeping a watchful eye out for insects and fish. It has a reddish band on its chest and a noticeable crest up top. The call of the kingfisher is distinctive: loud, rattling, and clicking. **Warblers** are often called the butterflies of the bird world. They are small, brightly colored, and move with gravity-defying ease. Contrary to their name, warblers are undistinguished singers, but they're great at collecting insects.

American Dipper

Belted Kingfisher

In the forests live brown creepers, mountain chickadees, and red- and white-breasted nuthatches. The **brown creeper** is difficult to spot because of the camouflage feathers that disguise it among tree trunks. Small, with a slender, curved beak, the creeper usually begins foraging for insects at the base of a tree and works its way up, clinging to the bark with razor-sharp claws. The **mountain chickadee** is another songbird with a delightful melody that sounds like "chick-adee-dee-dee." These tiny, friendly, hyperactive birds have dark caps and bibs, a gray or brown back, and a distinctive white eyebrow. They nest in woodpecker holes or other small tree holes. **Nuthatches** are the birds you'll see walking headfirst down a tree trunk—no simple feat. Also called upside-down birds, the red-breasted and white-breasted versions are aptly described by their names. They are partial to abandoned woodpecker holes.

Brown Creeper

Mountain Chickadee

Nuthatch

And let's not forget the **swift,** almost always found in flight above Yosemite Valley. These birds spend more time air-bound than any other land bird. When they do stop, they cling to vertical surfaces because their tiny feet are unsuitable for perches. Look up to see swifts flying between Yosemite's great granite walls. Both sexes look alike, and colors run from drab grays and browns to black and white.

In the Wawona region south of Yosemite Valley, you'll find the bushtit and wrentit, scrub jay, California thrasher, yellow warbler, lesser goldfinch, barn swallow, and ash-throated and rare willow flycatchers. The **yellow warbler** is the more colorful version of the warbler described above. **Swallows** are streamlined-looking birds with long, pointed wings. Swift in flight, they eat and drink on the fly. All are migratory, and some travel thousands of miles to the tropics each winter. **Flycatchers** are better known for their insect-hunting abilities than for distinctive markings. The **willow flycatcher** is a threatened species and has gray, brown, and olive plumage. All flycatchers are very territorial. **Goldfinches,** sometimes referred to as *wild canaries,* are gregarious birds, with bright colors and cheerful songs.

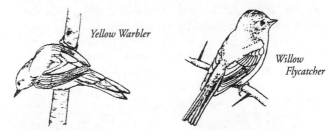

Yellow Warbler

Willow Flycatcher

Bushtits spend most of the year in flocks of about 20, constantly twittering at each other with a soft, lisping call. These acrobatic fliers are small, grayish birds with tiny bills. **Wrentits** are secretive birds—hard to see but easy to hear. They seldom venture far from home and prefer to live in chaparral or scrub thickets. Once mated, they form devoted pairs, constantly pruning and preening each other. When seen close together, they resemble a single ball of gray fluff. The **California thrasher** is one of several thrasher species, all of which have long tails and nest in low thickets. They forage on the ground and are accomplished singers, though not as notable as their distant cousins, the mockingbird and catbird.

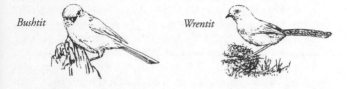

Bushtit

Wrentit

The high country of Yosemite and Sequoia & Kings Canyon attracts dozens more birds, drawn by altitude and mountain meadows, including the dark-eyed junco, kestrel, red-tailed hawk, killdeer, Williamson's sapsucker, Clark's nutcracker, and ptarmigan. **Juncos,** often referred to as *snowbirds,* are common visitors to bird feeders. Small and friendly, these birds resemble the sparrow, which also frequents this region. But the dark-eyed junco has a pink bill, white to bluish underbelly, and dark feathers from the crown down its back, and can usually be seen hopping along the ground in search of food. The **kestrel** is the smallest species of falcon. Like the falcon, it kills prey with a sharp bite to the neck, as opposed to hawks, which kill with their sharp claws. The **red-tailed hawk,** equipped with broad, rounded wings and a fan-shaped tail, soars effortlessly, using its keen eyesight to scan the area below for prey. The **killdeer**— named for its shrill call, is a performer, often feigning a broken wing to ward intruders off when they venture too near its nest. And no wonder—nests are little more than a shallow depression in the ground lined with pebbles. Adult killdeer have two black bands across their throats, while chicks have one.

Junco

Killdeer

Sapsuckers are specialized woodpeckers that extract the sap from trees with their brush-tipped tongues after drilling holes with their beaks. They also eat insects attracted to the sap. The **Williamson's sapsucker** strongly resembles the northern flicker described above, minus the red mustache. **Nutcrackers** are bold cousins of the crow family. **Clark's nutcrackers** specialize in prying seeds from pinecones and make forests their stamping grounds. In late summer and fall, the birds begin hoarding seeds for winter, tucking them in a pouch under their tongue during transport to slopes, where they poke holes in the ground and bury their treasure. A single nutcracker can hide 30,000 seeds. More remarkable is the fact that they remember where the stock is buried by the position of nearby landmarks, even when the ground is covered with snow. Clark's nutcracker resembles a crow, with a gray head and body and black wings tipped with white. Finally, the **ptarmigan** is a unique bird, well adapted to changing seasons in cold climates. These small, stocky grouse have mottled brown feathers in summer to help camouflage them against the rocky mountaintops where they live, but the feathers turn pure white in winter to match the snow. Like all grouse, ptarmigans have feathered legs, and in winter their feet are also covered with feathers. During the spring mating season, males sport a vibrant red comb and strut in short flights while cackling, all to attract a mate.

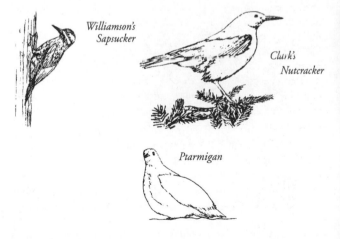

Williamson's Sapsucker

Clark's Nutcracker

Ptarmigan

In addition to the above birds, Hammond's flycatcher, Cassin's finch, common flicker, pine sparrow, chipping sparrow, white-crowned sparrow, and violet-green swallow are all prevalent in the high country.

MAMMALS

Mammals in these parks are not as commonly found as birds, but for some reason they're a lot more fun to spot. Most common are the mule deer, raccoon, squirrel, chipmunk, fox, coyote, and black bear. At higher elevations, you may also see Belding ground squirrels and Douglas's squirrels, yellow-bellied marmots, pikas, pine martens, badgers, mountain lions, bobcats, porcupines, long-tailed weasels, striped and spotted skunks, and northern water shrew.

Mule deer are most frequently spotted grazing in meadows at dawn and dusk. Although they seem gentle enough, mule deer should be treated with the same reverence accorded any wild animal: Give them a wide berth and, of course, refrain from feeding them. Many injuries have been recorded against humans who attempt to get close or feed them. The mule deer is named for its large, mule-like ears, and adults can weigh up to 200 pounds, surviving on a mix of grasses, leaves, tender twigs, and herbs. Males grow antlers for use during the mating season. And no, it is not true that the age of a male deer can be gauged by counting the points on its antlers.

Mule Deer

A variety of members of the squirrel family reside in this region, including chipmunks and marmots. The most common is the **California gray squirrel,** often seen in trees with its gray coat and bushy tail. The **California ground squirrel** is a brown animal with white speckles that prefers living in burrows. The **Sierra chickaree** is a reddish-colored tree squirrel that chews on pinecones and frequently makes a squeaking noise. **Douglas's squirrel,** common in Sequoia, is an olive-to-rust or gray color, with a reddish underbelly. At higher elevations, the **Belding ground squirrel** is most easily distinguished when it's seated—its erect posture resembles a stake driven into the ground. There are at least five different varieties of **chipmunks** in this region. Smaller than squirrels, they're quick and love to chatter, especially when scolding those who venture too near. Chipmunks range in color from reddish-brown to brownish-gray, and all varieties have four stripes running the length of their backs. At higher elevations, you'll find the yellow-bellied **marmot.** Resembling woodchucks, they regularly sunbathe and can tease visitors into believing they are tame. They're not. Adult marmots appear yellow-ish-brown, weigh up to 5 pounds, reach 15 to 18 inches in length, emit a high-pitched shrill as a warning, and live beneath rock piles or tree roots.

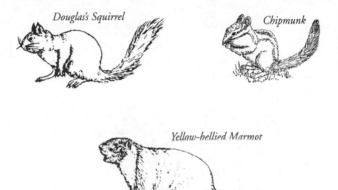

Douglas's Squirrel

Chipmunk

Yellow-bellied Marmot

The **porcupine** is a unique rodent. These short, stock-legged creatures are covered from head to toe with quills that detach at the touch, piercing whoever or whatever touches them. Each animal carries about 30,000 quills that serve as a serious deterrent to all but the stupidest predators. Porcupines sleep during the day and forage at night, curling into a ball when approached by a would-be predator. In spring, females produce one offspring, which is born with soft quills (thankfully) that harden within minutes. **Pikas** look like a cross between a rodent and a hare, and actually are distant relatives of the rabbit family. Pikas have oversized ears, although they're proportionately much smaller than those found on their cousins, and live in colonies above the tree line throughout the West. They scamper over rocks and emit a high-pitched squeal whenever a predator is sighted.

Porcupine   *Pika*

Raccoons are considered pests in suburbia, but in the wild they are shy nocturnal animals, easily spotted by their ringed tail and the appearance of a black mask across their eyes. Some are no bigger than a large house cat, but males can grow to be 3 feet in length and may weigh more than 40 pounds. These animals are adaptive, eating everything from fish and small rodents to fruit, nuts, and earthworms.

Raccoon

The parks contain a large number of weasel-family members, including badgers, martens, skunks, and what most people know as weasels. The **long-tailed weasel** can reach 16 inches in length. Usually brown with a white underbelly, in winter it can turn all white, while retaining a black tip to its tail. The badger and marten are distant cousins of the weasel. **Badgers** can reach up to 2 feet in length and weigh up to 25 pounds. This heavy, short-legged animal has black feet, black and white face markings, and coarse yellowish-gray fur. The **pine marten** is a fast, agile climber preferring high mountain forests. It is sometimes mistaken for a squirrel as it bounds from limb to limb, probably chasing a red squirrel, its favorite dinner. If you're not familiar with skunks, consider yourself fortunate. Best known for the awful scent they release when scared or under attack, skunks are otherwise cute, fluffy animals with distinctive black-and-white markings. Most common is the **striped skunk,** its white-on-black stripe running from nose to tail tip. The **spotted skunk** is more rare, but lives in Sequoia & Kings Canyon National Parks.

Badger

Striped Skunk

Foxes, coyotes, black bears, bobcats, and mountain lions also inhabit this region. Most avoid crowds and shun humans, but coyotes and black bears are frequently spotted in the middle of Yosemite Valley, where they rely on the misguided benevolence of humans who feed them. **Coyotes** resemble dogs, with long gray fur and bushy tails. They feed primarily on small rodents, and the occasional fawn, and grow to weigh between 25 and 30 pounds. One of the coyote's most distinctive traits is its howl, a long, haunting call that some consider frightening. The **black bear** is the largest mammal in these parks. It is often confused with the grizzly bear, which is much larger and much more fearsome. Incidents involving black bears usually occur due to improper food storage. *Never* feed bears, and by no means should you walk toward them. Observe from a safe distance. Despite their names, black bears can also be brown, blond, and cinnamon colored. Adult black bears grow to 250 to 500 pounds, and larger ones have been recorded. They are omnivores, eating both meat and vegetation, and they've proved very adaptable to hot dogs, hamburgers, and cookies. Unfortunately, once they become dependent on human food, these bears can prove bold and determined to continue their new diet. At this point, they must be trapped and killed by park rangers. Therefore, you *must* follow food-storage regulations.

Coyote

Black Bear

Foxes, bobcats, and mountain lions are less frequently spotted in the parks, especially the latter two. The most common fox is the **gray fox,** with its bushy tail, reddish-gray coat, and black paws. Members of the dog family, they look larger than they actually are—average weight is 10 pounds. Foxes are skillful hunters, and eat rodents, berries, rabbits, and insects. **Bobcats** inhabit Sequoia & Kings Canyon National Parks. They are nocturnal and resemble a large cat, with a black-spotted tawny coat. The "bob" refers to their stub of a tail, a feature shared with their close relative, the lynx. Adults max out at about 20 pounds, and while much smaller than the next predator on our list, bobcats can kill deer many times their size. They are masters of the slow hunt—methodical, solitary, and patient. **Mountain lions** shy away from any human contact, so seeing one is extremely rare. These large cats can reach 5 feet in length. Their fur ranges from tawny to gray, their tails tipped with black. Solitary predators who prefer elk and deer, in lean times they'll settle for a porcupine or skunk.

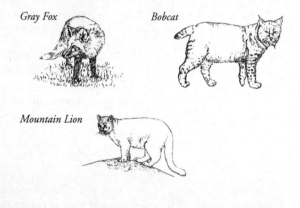

Gray Fox

Bobcat

Mountain Lion

4 The Ecosystem

Quite often, the ravages of nature are the forces of change, and such has been the case in these national parks. Recent rock slides and floods have reestablished nature's supremacy, and preservation efforts and long-term studies have been underway for more than a decade.

In Yosemite, the return of the peregrine falcon was heralded as a milestone. When bird-watchers counted three nesting pairs and five offspring in 1996, the news traveled across the nation.

Considerable attention is going to restoring meadows, limiting trails, and bringing back native plants pushed out by the impact of humans. The valley has seen the reseeding of a black-oak forest along the bikeway between Yosemite Village and Yosemite Falls.

Large boulders placed in the Merced River long ago by settlers and early park managers changed the course of the waterway and created unnatural swimming holes. These are being removed, and the river is being allowed to pursue its own direction. Volunteers are working to repair damage done by hikers who step off the trails.

In Sequoia & Kings Canyon, fire management has been a major concern since the 1960s, when the park policies began to be questioned. Early on, tree preservation was the cornerstone of park policy, so natural wildfires were squelched whenever possible. But after a noticeable decline in tree germination, research determined that fire is necessary—it dries out the cones to release their seeds, burns underbrush, and clears openings in the canopy for sunlight to reach the seedlings. In 1968, an unprecedented fire-management program began that allows some natural wildfires to burn, sets prescribed burns, and suppresses unwanted blazes. Consequently, over the past 20 years, the increase in the regeneration rate of giant sequoias has been noticeable.

Other environmental concerns for the park include air quality and drought. Unfortunately, Sequoia & Kings Canyon is located near California's smoggy Central Valley, and has the most chronically polluted air of the Western parks, often obscuring what would otherwise be superlative views. In 2004, the EPA designated Sequoia & Kings Canyon as an area in which ozone pollution was a risk to human health. Ozone pollution also weakens the trees, so that when natural drought comes along, these damaged trees often die.

Dealing with the issues facing both parks requires time, money, and commitment—all high hurdles. Partnerships have been formed with foundations, nature conservancies, and even oil companies, to provide funding for study and restoration. But the single biggest issue for both parks remains overcrowding.

For most of the 20th century and into the 21st, the parks have walked a tenuous line between increasing visitation and consistent management of visitation. Research has changed some policies, and experience is changing others. Meanwhile, park personnel hope that educational efforts being made on all fronts will continue to preserve the parks for future generations of nature enthusiasts.

Index

See also Accommodations and Restaurant indexes below.

ACCOMMODATIONS

RESTAURANTS

Frommer's® Complete Guides

The only guide independent travelers need to make smart choices, avoid rip-offs, get the most for their money, and travel like a pro.

Frommer's®

 WILEY

Available at bookstores everywhere.

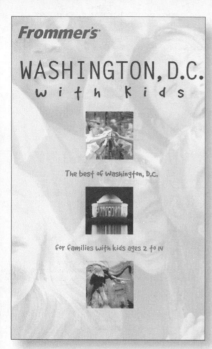

THE NEW TRAVELOCITY GUARANTEE

EVERYTHING YOU BOOK WILL BE RIGHT, OR WE'LL WORK WITH OUR TRAVEL PARTNERS TO MAKE IT RIGHT, RIGHT AWAY.

*To drive home the point,
we're going to use the word "right" in every single sentence.*

Let's get right to it. Right to the meat! Only Travelocity guarantees everything about your booking will be right, or we'll work with our travel partners to make it right, right away. Right on!

Here's a picture taken smack dab right in the middle of Antigua, where the guarantee also covers you.

The guarantee covers all but one of the items pictured to the right.

For example, what if the ocean view you booked actually looks out at a downright ugly parking lot? You'd be right to call – we're there for you. And no one in their right mind would be pleased to learn the rental car place has closed and left them stranded. Call Travelocity and we'll help get you back on the right track.

Now, you may be thinking, "Yeah, right, I'm so sure." That's OK; you have the right to remain skeptical. That is until we mention help is always right around the corner. Call us right off the bat, knowing that our customer service reps are there for you 24/7. Righting wrongs. Left and right.

Now if you're guessing there are some things we can't control, like the weather, well you're right. But we can help you with most things – to get all the details in righting,* visit **travelocity.com/guarantee**.

*Sorry, spelling things right is one of the few things not covered under the guarantee.

I'd give my right arm for a guarantee like this, although I'm glad I don't have to.

travelocity
You'll never roam alone.

IF YOU BOOK IT, IT SHOULD BE THERE.

Only Travelocity guarantees it will be, or we'll work with our travel partners to make it right, right away. So if you're missing a balcony or anything else you booked, just call us 24/7. **1-888-TRAVELOCITY.**

travelocit

You'll never roam alo